T0193737

GIRL TRIBES

The Teen Girl's Guide to Surviving and Thriving
in our Media Marketing World

HELEN ROE

BALBOA.
PRESS

A DIVISION OF HAY HOUSE

Balboa Press books may be ordered through booksellers or by contacting:

Balboa Press
A Division of Hay House
1663 Liberty Drive
Bloomington, IN 47403
www.balboapress.com.au
1 (877) 407-4847

Because of the dynamic nature of the Internet, any web addresses or links contained in this book may have changed since publication and may no longer be valid. The views expressed in this work are solely those of the author and do not necessarily reflect the views of the publisher, and the publisher hereby disclaims any responsibility for them.

The author of this book does not dispense medical advice or prescribe the use of any technique as a form of treatment for physical, emotional, or medical problems without the advice of a physician, either directly or indirectly. The intent of the author is only to offer information of a general nature to help you in your quest for emotional and spiritual well-being. In the event you use any of the information in this book for yourself, which is your constitutional right, the author and the publisher assume no responsibility for your actions.

Any people depicted in stock imagery provided by Thinkstock are models, and such images are being used for illustrative purposes only. Certain stock imagery © Thinkstock.

Print information available on the last page.

ISBN: 978-1-5043-0353-8 (sc)
ISBN: 978-1-5043-0354-5 (e)

Balboa Press rev. date: 07/29/2016

To Sarah and Ava, my inspiration.
Keep shining my loves.

before we start...

Hey! I'm so excited you're here! I've been so looking forward to meeting you. It's a noisy media mayhem of a world out there. Why don't you come on in, sit down and relax for a moment?

Welcome to *GirlTribes,* your guide to surviving and thriving in our media marketing world. Not as a clone. Not as a walking brand. But as the original you.

How are you? Busy I bet, so thank you for taking the time to pick up this book. I'm glad you did because I'd like to take you on a journey to show you how we all live our lives through the magnetic mesmerising marketing lens. It's honest, it's connected and it's an opportunity you don't want to miss.

Media marketing is a big part of your world. You are constantly connected. I've been 'behind the scenes' with an incredible overview of this wonderful wide-open-to-possibilities world of marketing for longer that I care to remember. Do this, watch that. Try this, eat that. Wear this, look like that. Behave like this, react like that. Got a problem? We have the solution. It's exhausting, right?

Don't you just wish they'd make up their mind? One minute you're told to be unique. The next it's all about buying [insert brand spanking new miracle product] to fit in. Enough! Get ready to start thinking creatively, don your superhero persona and confidently take your own comfortable stance in this world. *GirlTribes* is your guide map to making your own informed decisions. Backed with real-life insights from smart girls just like you.

My wish for you after reading this book is that you'll feel stronger and more confident to trust your own inner guidance. You'll deep down recognise and appreciate your own self-worth. And you'll feel less pressure to be someone else other than you.

Sound good? Great!

reading this book will...

:: Help you make sense of the way marketing pulls you in and the non-stop media noise telling you what's best.

:: Support and empower you to make smarter, more informed decisions about what you buy and why.

:: Enable you to blast through any doubts and fears that media triggers within you.

:: Provide you with tips and tricks to bypass the yucky stuff and use meaningful marketing to make your mark.

:: Encourage you to stay curious and question media marketing, confidently making the best decisions for you.

So why listen to me? Firstly, I'm not here to lecture. So it's all good - you can relax. Yes, I'm a parent to two gorgeous daughters, but I realise you will drop this book like a hot potato if you think it's going to be a long list of to-dos. Instead, how about thinking of it like having an open-minded conversation with your favourite aunt? Awesome – I'm glad we're on the same page.

Full disclosure. As one of those marketing people myself, I used to eat marketing strategy for breakfast. I spent my university days and all of my professional career to date submerged in A-list marketing strategies (AKA selling stuff in increasingly creative ways) for global brands. I also speak at conferences and workshops on the subject of marketing, and to anyone else who will listen! So yes, I'm from 'the other side', but I'm here now, on yours. And I'm ready to spill all the dirty little secrets of the marketing industry and how they get you to buy, buy, buy. (Hint: it's not always pretty). To prove I'm human (and still partial to a good ad), I should probably mention I've got a *slight* handbag affliction and I own a pair of red heels I've never worn. More on that later.

I can't (and wouldn't) tell you what to do, but what I can share with you is ahas and oh-I-sees to help *you* decide for yourself. Make choices that will get you feeling proud and reaching your fullest potential.

Ready to challenge and change your own corner of the world? Let's go!

Helen
xx

how to read this book

Follow the text from left to right, top to bottom, then... OK no, seriously though, the way to get the most out of this book is to read it in sequence. That way, some later parts of the book make more sense. Each chapter builds on the other. It's a bit like getting to know someone. You start with hello and some nice chit-chat. You don't expect to hear their life story in your first conversation together.

First up, we meet Monika, our metaphor for marketing in this book. She's our leading girl. In each chapter, you'll get to know more about her, her behaviour and why she does what she does. It's a great way of getting up to speed on the latest marketing goings-on without all the jargon.

To help you get the most out of this book, I've added some light-hearted Move Over Monika reflections for you. These inspirational activities and challenges will help you put into practice your ahas. I've included them in every chapter after we've talked about a particular concept or idea. I highly recommend using these reflections to strengthen your self-confidence and 'I've got this' muscles.

There's also Playsheet activities. That's right. Words without action are meaningless so put your insights into action with some fun, doable activities. You can also access your Playsheets plus bonus goodies in the GirlTribes Action Kit online. Download it free on my website at www.helenroe.com/girltribes. Your GirlTribes Action Kit is full of extra printables to help you get the most out of the book and activate a smarter, more confident media-savvy you. Print them out and post them on your wall or somewhere you will see them regularly.

OK then, that's about it. Your friend awaits. Monika is dying to meet you. Let's dive in!

* * * * *

Contents

Part 1

AHA, I GET IT!

Eye-Opening Awareness

Chapter 1

Meet Monika – The It-Girl

Be humble enough to know you are not better than anybody else,
but wise enough to know that you are different.

Please step forward and accept your award. As part of the teen generation, I now pronounce you the most influential consumer group. In. The. World. *Congratulations!* Here's your key to connectivity, creation and changing the world.

Wow! That's some title. The most influential consumer group. In the world. Well, one of. I omitted 'one of', but that's a minor detail. Did you have any idea how much power you had? Maybe not. You just showed up online, connected, never having experienced the pre-internet world. Still, it's very impressive and I'm a tad jealous.

Now, wait up a sec. Before you think I'm going to reminisce about the good ol' days, walking barefoot to school (OK, that wasn't my generation, but a couple of generations before), I'm not. Digital natives, extended millennials, generation like, generation connected, extended Gen Z – these are just some of the titles you are fondly called. But I'm not here to go on about how great you have it either.

♥ In a world saturated with noisy media and marketing messages, it's easy to lose sight of who you are and how you are perceived by others. In this chapter, you'll meet and get to know the It-Girl Monika, the personality who makes the world of marketing go around. She's the analogy I'll use to explain the whole concept of marketing and she'll keep us company throughout this book. You'll learn how Monika can have a big influence on the way you see yourself.

So many mixed messages. Subconsciously taking it all in. Getting used to all the noise. Media everywhere. Sometimes you don't notice it. Other times you do. Some days you feel great. And others, well, you might feel like you don't 'have enough' or aren't the 'right look' or can't 'fit in'. Even if you're not on social media or watching TV, you still can't avoid it. On public transport, walking down the street, putting your rubbish in the bin, even using a public toilet! It's a fact. Marketing messages everywhere. There's no escape. Research states we are exposed to these messages up to 5,000 times a day![1]

Eat this, drink that. Look like this, wear that. Watch this, ponder that. Go here, visit there. What's a girl to do? From so-called perfection with air-brushed models to cool kids flirting and feasting on fast food at the beach, we see ultimate lifestyles and life experiences play out before our eyes.

It's exciting, it's entertaining, it's informative, it's inspirational! It's irritating, it's annoying, it's pushy, it's exhausting! You grow tired of everyone telling you what's best. Welcome to the world of marketing.

Amidst all the marketing noise, it's time to take control of how you do things. Confidently make your own choices. Be your own voice. Even use marketing to make a meaningful difference. On our journey together, we're going to get to know Monika a lot more. Just like you, Monika has good and not-so-good (*OK, real bad!*) days. We'll take a look at both. We'll look at how the choices you make fit into Monika's marketing world. It'll be eye-opening to get a glimpse from an insider. And I think you're both going to get along just fine.

---

[1] Walker-Smith, J, Yankelovich research, Yankelovich Partners (2007)

Why GirlTribes?

Tribes have been around for millions of years. Tribes are people who connect for a common interest. It's in our nature to want to feel a sense of belonging or familiarity and be part of a something. A tribe.

When girls find like-minded kindred spirits, they are supported to be who they really want to be. No pretence and no pressure. Great things happen. Every girl should have the support of a tribe behind her. One that you choose to be part of, not one that a brand persuaded you into following.

I use the term 'tribe' almost daily in my work in marketing. I first heard it from Seth Godin, one of the world's most successful authors and bloggers, who has changed the way the world sees marketing. He is marketing's middle name. In the world of marketing, a tribe refers to a target market or specific group of people or consumers who a marketer wants to connect with.

GirlTribes is the coming together of two incredible global forces, teen girls and tribes. United in common interest, solidarity and sisterhood. Supported and strong, confident in your ability to achieve what you want. And do your thing.

Alone we can do so little, together we can do so much.
~ Helen Keller

Meet Monika, the marketing It-Girl

I bet you've heard of her, or maybe you met her already. She's the one that everyone knows or wishes they knew. She's always at the centre of things. Popular, pretty and smart to boot. She's always friendly and has a kind word to say. There's that *something* about her presence, people take notice. She is *the* girl everyone wants to be.

If you haven't met her yet, I'd like to introduce you. Meet Monika. Monika is the marketing It-Girl. She's the medium that makes everything in a marketing world tick. Monika is the girl in the ad you see on TV. She's that girl in cool gym gear in your favourite magazine.

She's that girl holding a smoothie at the trendy café. And she's that girl-in-the-know telling you 'you don't want to miss this' (which, you might have noticed, makes you feel left out and lonely).

I'll talk lots more about Monika as we go. You'll get to know each other better and learn how to get on. Maybe even be good friends. Just to be clear, I'm introducing Monika as a metaphor for marketing to help convey the many personalities, pros and cons, ups and downs of living in a marketing world. She makes things a bit more interesting!

Marketing is more than just advertising

Advertising is one of the more popular forms of marketing and how Monika most frequently shows up in the world. But marketing is way more than just advertising and selling. Wikipedia says marketing is 'an integrated process through which companies build strong customer relationships and create value for their customers and for themselves'. It's a combination of many steps that focus on the customer. We will talk more about these steps throughout the book.

If you'd like the professor-style definition on marketing then the Chartered Institute of Marketing captures it well by describing marketing as 'the management process responsible for identifying, anticipating and satisfying customer requirements profitably'. In other words, giving customers what they want, while also making a profit. It includes things like looking at the way customers behave, researching what people want and need, deciding what groups of people they're going to target, analysing how the audience they're talking to is made up, making sure everything they do has the same vibe (in the biz, we call this 'branding' and it's more than just the pretty design), building relationships, thinking about the price of what they're selling, giving information about the product itself, dreaming up creative interesting ways to promote what they're selling, deciding how to get the product to the customer, and much more. (*Phew!*) All of these have specific marketing terms, but for now, all you need to know is that a lot goes on behind a big brand. A lot! Monika is one multi-talented girl with many skills. Advertising is just one of them.

Marketing is simple, clear, effective communication that has a purpose.
It's how a business survives by getting the word out. It is
the art of getting people to make up their minds.

Why do I need to know this Monika anyway?

You are strong, smart and make your own independent decisions,
right? Good, I thought so. If you're keen to make your own decisions,
awareness is key. Once you're aware why Monika exists and how she
works, you can make *informed* decisions about everything - from what
you put into your mouth for breakfast to how you feel about yourself
when your head hits the pillow at night.

Getting to know Monika will help you navigate the many decisions
and sometimes overload of messages, ads and reminders that you face
every single day. Remember, during your day, you see thousands of
messages, whether you're conscious of it or not. These messages are
making up your mind for you. Unless, you are aware of them and know
how to handle them. Even if that sometimes means doing nothing.

What is Monika really like?

Monika, AKA marketing, knows what she wants to say. She is clear
and confident and great at communication. It's very likely she's on the
debating team. She's brilliant at persuading you of her point of view.
You may not always be interested or even in agreement with what
she has to say. But she talks anyway. Monika loves to chat and share
pictures. She makes you feel all kinds of crazy sometimes. One minute
she has you giggling, the next she has you feeling insecure, vulnerable
and wanting so badly to fit in. Yes, Monika makes an impact.

Move Over Monika

Have you met Monika? Where and how often? Be completely honest and about your impression of her so far. Can you not get enough of her? Does she guide your decisions? Does she drive you nuts or annoy you? There's no right or wrong answer here. This is purely for awareness and to help you both get to know each other.

I asked some girls like you their impression of Monika and her marketing world. Here's what they had to say.

'Marketing is about communication through gorgeous models. The images the media portray of girls my age is that they are sexy and slim, mad about boys, beautiful and popular. Sometimes when I see advertisements with girls my age having fun, I feel alone and boring. I still unconsciously strive for the ideal body standards.'
~ *Jessica, twelve*

'Marketing is about selling and communication. When I see advertisements with girls my age in them I automatically compare myself. I end up feeling deflated or not good enough. It makes me feel bad that I'm not good enough to be doing these things. I usually see girls on Instagram my age with thousands of followers, who are absolutely stunning and have the nicest clothes, makeup, boyfriend... everything. I feel like it's my responsibility to be reaching the same goals as them. It's more of a disappointment in myself than jealousy or feeling left out.'
~ *Izabella, sixteen*

'When I see advertisements with girls my age in them it makes me feel disgusted and jealous. The pictures look so perfect. But they have been Photoshopped. Everything is edited and fake.'
~ *Anna, fifteen*

'The messages I see in the media are that happy successful girls are thin and dress to show off their figure. Successful girls look a 'certain way' and listen to a certain type of cool music. Sometimes I feel like I want to be them, but then later I think I shouldn't do that. I should be myself and believe in myself.'
~ *Becky, thirteen*

'I don't believe everything I see in the media. However, things they say do stick in the back of my mind even if I don't think they're true.'
~ *Anna, fifteen*

Where do you see Monika?

Monika is everywhere. Yes, really. When you get up in the morning and pick up your phone (*shhh, I'm telling no-one!*) she's on there. She's sharing messages and stories and pictures with you. Advertising appears in many formats. Sometimes you can clearly tell an ad is an ad. Other times, it's in the form of sponsorship of an event, like a music concert, or a 'brand endorsement' where a celebrity is wearing or using a particular product. Other times you might see a sponsored post on your Facebook or Instagram feed and it's like Monika is inside your head.

Truth is she is! Monika has been tracking your likes and dislikes so closely, she might even appear to know you better than you know yourself.

When you're having your breakfast she's probably on some packaging, smiling, promoting the latest new must-have *thing*. Flick on the TV and she's warbling on about *something or other* before your programme starts. Prefer to flick through a magazine or the newspaper? She'll be there too. Talking about family issues, pets, food, homes and the like.

Unless you're asleep or hiding under a rock, Monika is usually around. She has lots to say. She's kind of supportive, but needs encouragement and reminding to talk about what *you* want to talk about. When you interact with Monika, through a magazine or by commenting or liking a post on social media, searching on your phone or clicking an image online, she gets to know your likes and dislikes. Every single interaction. Every click. Every like. That's when she really starts to work her charm. Your friendship has begun.

Is Monika in my head?

Have you ever felt like Monika knows you so well she's inside your head? Totally normal. Monika has just tapped a sensitive spot, a niggly nerve. We all have them. Something we don't feel quite *woohoo!* about. Monika is excellent at finding out what will strike a nerve with you. (It's known as market research for your 'pain point'.)

First, she will get inside your head in a nice way. She has a way of identifying your weak spot, empathising, then making you feel that you can rely on her to be there. Almost like you need her around or can't be yourself without her. She is your friend some days. When she first starts to figure out the way you think, she'll be super friendly, asking questions and agreeing a lot with what you have to say.

Gradually, you'll notice she gets a little bossy. Once Monika gets to know you, she'll start to comment the way you *should* be dressing, eating, exercising, whatever. If you notice, she'll always have a solution for you to *be better.* She likes you to use her advice and choose her solution, the item or shop that she recommends. This is Monika (AKA marketing) at her best.

Now, sometimes that product or service or brand or place that Monika recommends will be good for you. It might be just what you need. That new hairstyle that makes your eyes just *wow!* Or that book that you can lose yourself in and escape into another world. That's Monika at her best.

But when is enough really *enough?* Monika doesn't have an off button. She also doesn't know the difference between when you really really *want* something and when you really really *need* something. This is a super important distinction.

Monika works from a place of want only. Monika wants you to have everything. Monika wants the best for you, sure, but Monika wants her version of what's the best for you.

You can get advice for amazing new products. You can choose carefully if you'd truly like 'the next big thing'. But only *you* know what's best for *you*. And how you know that is by learning and understanding more about what it is that makes you tick.

Monika is only in your head if you let her. Some space and time apart is a good thing. You just need to know how to tell her it's time for a time-out. Confidently and calmly. Monika will sense if you're not sure about this. She excels and performs her best marketing moves when she taps into your vulnerabilities and insecurities.

That doesn't mean you have to hide these parts of you. We all have insecurities and being vulnerable is simply showing you are a human. You're not a robot. But in terms of getting along with Monika, bearing those vulnerable parts requires some tweaking. A bit like when you have to tell a friend a truth they might not want to hear. You dread saying it, but saying it is better for you both in the long run. There are a few simple steps you can take to ensure Monika gets the message clearly. Don't worry. I'll show you how in the next chapter.

Move Over Monika

What was the last thing Monika showed you in the media? Think for a moment. Recall how you felt when you listened, watched or read what she was saying. Was it a picture, a TV ad, a social media post? Did you feel pressure to agree? Or did you dismiss it as not relevant to you? What kind of things did you say to yourself?

Write it down, or capture it in a picture or quote and share it with #GirlTribes on Instagram.

Keep up the great work with your *Move Over Monika* reflections. If you're looking for more inspiration and ideas to support and guide you, go to www.helenroe.com/girltribes for your free GirlTribes Action Kit. It's full of extra goodies.

Next up, it's time to get to know the original awesome you. We'll go a little deeper to reveal some hidden gems. Get ready to shine.

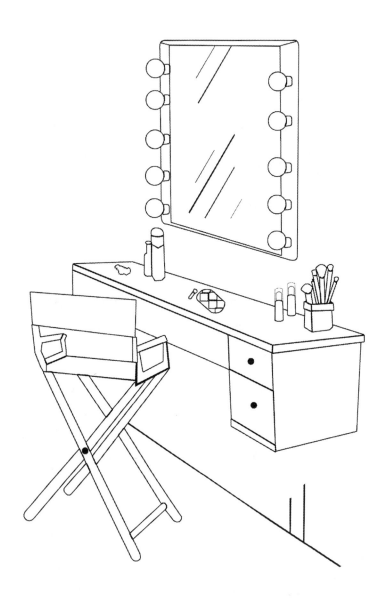

Chapter 2

Your Exclusive Personal Brand

Be yourself.
An original is worth more than a copy.

What are you worth? A million dollars? Ten million? A billion?! You are of course priceless, wonderfully unique in your own way. You are a limited edition. And you cannot put a price on that!

Honestly though, have you ever thought about your self-worth? The level of confidence and satisfaction you have with yourself? That sense of how deserving you are. It can be quite a challenge!

In Monika's marketing world, she is acutely aware of any hidden insecurities you might have. Even if you appear confident, she will find a way to provoke doubt in your identity, that level of comfortable acceptance you have in yourself. This is why it's so important for you to get clear on your worth and remind yourself of it daily.

♥ In this chapter, we'll explore your personal core values. Your very own Personal Brand. These are the measurements of your true worth, not the short-term self-esteem boosters from your latest success or failure. You'll learn how powerful your Personal Brand really is. These superpowers help you navigate Monika and her marketing moves – big time.

For a long time, my self-worth was associated with my education, my accomplishments and achievements. For sure, these areas helped me feel good about myself; I was on the right track to being the best version of myself. I measured up. But there were times I fell short of this measurement. I had a lower value of myself in those times, because I didn't 'achieve' a particular grade, make a particular team or look a certain way.

These fluctuations in my self-worth caused many a crappy day. I'm sure you can relate. We all have these days. The question is: why do we put ourselves through all that when this 'measuring up' is skewed in the first place?! These self-inflicted measurements I adopted once upon time were unsustainable and unhealthy. Let's save you that pain.

Avoid falling into the not-measuring-up trap. Here's a reminder of some of the common yet dangerous ways that you might find yourself measuring your value.

♥ Hanging out with certain people to feel good

You have no control over other people. You do have control over who you choose to spend your time with. Both online and offline. But hanging out with the cool gang, the crazy gang or whomever you choose to help you feel braver, bolder, bigger, is like chasing the horizon. It's always moving and you will never get close to it.

Action:

Compliments and praise from others is great, but start with your own approval and acceptance first. If you're constantly looking to others, you'll never receive enough of what you're looking for. Take a moment to list five things you appreciate about yourself.

♥ The number of likes or followers you have on social media

I'm sure you know of girls who measure their self-worth by their online status. Perhaps they don't even realise they're doing it! This is a dangerous game and one that leads to disappointment. The amount of followers or likes you have will never be enough and you'll always be comparing and basing your worth on other people's opinions.

Action:

Enjoy online friendships, liking and commenting, if that's part of your social scene. But your online presence is not an indication of your worth and who you truly are. Notice what your thoughts are when you see someone online with more friends or followers than you. Notice how you react and what you feel when this happens.

♥   How you look and dress

This is one of the most common self-worth barometer myths. I've certainly experienced this one and I'm sure you have at some stage too. But how you look and dress is not where your value lies. Never judge a book by its cover and all that. Of course, we're not talking wearing last week's spag-bol-stained top here. You can have standards! It's more about having the latest and the greatest. The look. The way to dress. According to Monika. Yes. All that. She'll target your insecurities when you are most vulnerable.

Action:

Decide how you want to dress and what you want to look like according to what makes you feel [insert your own feeling here]. (Hint: comfortable, happy, creative, colourful, smart, classic, fun, unique are all good options here.) Of course, school uniforms can limit that on some days, but you know what I mean!

♥   What you achieve

This used to rank high on my list as how I judged my self-worth and I still wrangle with it at times. You associate your self-worth with achieving the next thing on your list. You will feel deserving once you 'get there' and accomplish your next big goal. Woah! Here we go again.

Chasing that horizon. There will always be another thing on that list. It's like a moving target, impossible to hit!

Action:

Have you ever felt you'll be smarter, fitter, skinnier, taller, older or whatever, when you do that one thing? And then, when you do that thing, you realise there's another thing! And another. Think of a time you achieved something great, but didn't stop to celebrate before moving onto the next thing, and how that affected your feelings of self-worth.

Achievements and accomplishments are awesome. They do make us feel good about ourselves, I admit. Just be careful not to measure your self-worth solely on your achievements though, because it's conditional. It's temporary. It would mean attaching a belief of yourself to achieving something else. It's a bit like saying 'I will be a great person when I [insert thing you need to do]'. The problem with this is, you will experience major ups and downs. And you will always play safe and avoid challenging activities where you might not feel 'ready' or where you think you might fail, just so your self-worth stays intact.

Using Monika for validation

Knowing your value and uniqueness is one thing. Living by them is more powerful still. Use your gifts and talents. Be a living example to others so that they too can recognise their own value. When you know who you are and accept the real you, you will naturally build a strong sense of self and self-worth.

Sounds straightforward enough. Then we bring Monika into the mix and it gets a little more complicated. When we seek value from someone or something else, that's when Monika and her marketing mob start to really influence. You get caught up in that search for being *enough*. It's great to receive nice gifts, wear gorgeous clothes and have lots of followers on social media. These are all external devices through which you express yourself (or maybe not).

This 'stuff' does not determine who you really are. Nor does the number of likes you get for a selfie, the number of Instagram followers you have or any other social media measurement. Sure, it's instant gratification and feels good. It's fun. It's a form of compliment after all. Monika and her marketing friends like to encourage you to think that owning more 'stuff' is a measure of your worthiness. The more you have/buy/eat/spend, the happier you are. This, of course, is not the case.

When you have this awareness, you can be more open-minded about the choices you make. You can make smarter choices. Are you collecting more 'stuff' as a way to feel better about yourself or to keep up with external pressures? Keep reading, we can work through this together.

Spotting the signs

I used to compete a lot in athletics. I still love to run, but at a more sedentary pace! I was fast and my long legs carried me to the finish line in lightning speed. One of my first races as a toddler, the tiny tots, will forever be etched in my memory. Not for winning it but for the journey home in our yellow Renault 5. (It was a long time ago, what can I say?)

I vividly recall the red handbag. Sitting pretty on the trophy table where all the prizes gleamed and glistened like jewels. The fashionable red handbag was clearly first prize, followed not so closely by a doll of some kind. Boring. Then third prize. Well, I can't even remember what that was. That red handbag had my name all over it.

I ran my little heart out. After the race, still gulping for air, I proudly stepped up on the podium in first position (expertly hand-painted with a white number one). Next thing, I remember a doll being thrust into my hand. *That* hideous doll. My mouth dropped. The girl who came second clutched the red handbag, grinning like she'd won the lottery. What?! There'd been some kind of mistake.

'No, I don't care if I've won. I care about the red handbag!' I balled. This clearly was not going to be one of those 'it's not winning that matters, it's the taking part that counts' conversations I'm sure my mum would have preferred. 'But rosebud, you won the race', she whispered, 'And look, this doll is so beautiful'. I really didn't think so. I promptly threw her in the back seat of the car, folding my arms tightly to further emphasise the scowl I wore on my face for the whole journey home.

I had already pictured how grown-up I would be with that bag. So stylish. A 'big girl'. For me, it was a beautiful bag over a cute doll any day. Ha! Four years old and I was a handbag person. I still love a good handbag. I like particular brands too (even I'm not immune to great marketing). But the brands, the bags, they do not define me. So let's lean in, look a little closer and see what other gems we can find. It's time to get to know the real, limited edition, original you.

Move Over Monika

What age can you recall first having a sense of what you liked and who you wanted to be? Can you recall being adamant about the way you wore your hair? Your favourite lose-track-of-time activity? Think of at least three characteristics that described the younger you. These first traits are often great indicators of your personality and how you show up in the world.

When you know what you like, what moves you and what has meaning for you,
decisions become easier.
Life becomes easier.

And Monika becomes less persistent, less of an influencing factor in your life, even though she'll always be there. Discovering more about *you* is what you're here to do. And a big part of that is taking a look at your Personal Brand.

What exactly is a brand?

A brand is the story behind a product or service. It's a big part of Monika's image and she puts a lot of thought and effort into creating her brand. Her voice, her style, her values. It's more than just a logo or a brochure. It's heart and soul; the essence of the business she represents.

A brand connects you with the product on a deeper level. That doesn't mean you have to eat, live and breathe commitment to anyone but yourself. Think of it like this. When you Google a well-known person, what you see, the feeling you get about the person, that's their brand. It's not always something tangible that you can touch or feel. It's their reputation.

Today, we see a lot more people marketing themselves as brands. Personal brands. Celebrities, sporting heroes, singers and even YouTube sensations create successful careers from branding their own personalities. Connor Franta, who creates lifestyle vlogs and comedy skits has 5.4 million subscribers. Lilly Singh, otherwise known as iiSuperWomanii is a vlogger and comedian with 8.6 million subscribers. Bethany Mota vlogs on fashion and style to over 10 million subscribers. These personalities are great examples of Personal Branding at its best.

Even if you don't desire stardom and the stage, you too have your own Personal Brand. Your online interests and your actions are all traceable. It's up to you if you want to influence that. That last YouTube video you watched? Yes, Monika knows you love funny cat videos now. That top you bought on eBay? She even knows your size and colour preference. That like and comment you made on a friend of a friend's birthday pic on Instagram? All traceable back to you. Monika is watching you. (Don't freak out, she asks permission most of the time!)

Your Personal Brand is what people say about you after you leave the room.

Consciously creating your Digital Footprint

Whether you're aware of it or not, you have a Digital Footprint. This trail of data you leave online through the sites you visit, the comments you post, the images you like, the purchases you make etc. is there for everyone to see. It's permanent, like a tattoo. Your Digital Footprint is your reputation. Keep it clean. Monika and the marketing team use this to help them make decisions and better understand what to say to you. (It shapes their 'marketing message' as we call it.)

Consider another angle for now though. Picture your own Digital Footprint. What if a stranger was to get to know you purely through your Digital Footprint? Who do you think they would see? Would you like how they perceive you? Is this the real you? These are important questions to ask yourself. Use your Digital Footprint Playsheet to explore if your online and offline personalities match.

Great news if your personalities are matching. You are consistent and honest with yourself. If not, be gentle but curious. Which version of you do you prefer? Whichever one it is, be more of her.

your digital footprint

Your Digital Footprint, where you choose to hang out online, says a lot about you. Choose carefully.

Where can your friends find you online?
List the media types you use. (E.g. specific websites, apps, magazines, YouTube, Facebook, Instagram etc.)

What type of person do you want people to see online?
List the characteristics of the person others see of you on your online home. (E.g. always happy, honest, confident, very cool, sporty, outgoing, shy, fashionable etc.)

Is this how you are in your everyday real life?

Are you comfortable with this? If not, can you identify why?

How can you continue to create an authentic original Digital Footprint?

(E.g. avoiding comparisons, staying real and practicing what you post, choosing media that supports you in feeling good about yourself.)

Is brand loyalty worth it?

When you think of a brand, what comes to mind? A global brand like Nike, Apple or Coca-Cola, or perhaps something less well-known and local to your community. A brand is many things. What makes a brand special is the feeling it evokes in us when we see or recall it.

Think about your favourite brand. What is it that draws you to it? It has to be more than 'my friends like it'. How does it make you feel? Fashionable, sophisticated, cool, comfortable, confident, or something else? Your answers offer clues to help you later, when you will be creating your own Personal Brand.

If your favourite brand affects you in a positive way, this is a good thing. I personally love brands. I enjoy the familiarity, trust and reassurance of certain brands I like and use again and again. That means I'm 'brand-loyal' to certain brands. Some brands come and go, as my interests change. On the other hand, I've had some favourite brands for years including Nike (hey, I'm sporty), Apple and Kate Spade. However, I don't pledge my life or all my extra cash to these brands. I don't *become* them. They enhance how I express myself.

'I bought Converse because everyone else was wearing them. It's exciting but the people in ads make you feel like you want to be them.'
~ *Mikaela, fourteen*

'I tend to stick to my opinions no matter what other people think about them. However, I have bought some things that I've liked the look of that seemed fun and interesting.'
~ *Suzanne, fifteen*

Does your favourite brand enhance you in some way? This is the game changer. If you follow or use a brand to be someone other than who you really are, then we're talking brand-washing. That's a term I coined to explain how you get brain-washed by a brand telling you who to be and how to act. It's a bad place to start and it ends even worse. You lose your identity; become an external seeker of approval, looking outside of yourself for validation all the time. In summary, you become a marketer's dream. You and Monika will be best friends forever!

Don't get me wrong. It's OK to be brand-loyal. But like everything, in moderation. Monika loves you to be brand-loyal; just be aware *why* you love a particular brand. The more dependent you become on a brand to receive something like confidence, identity, or cool factor, the harder it is to resist Monika's marketing moves. You will fall hook, line and sinker for every marketing move she makes.

Nurture your Personal Brand

Your brand personality is a means of expressing yourself. It's your style, your tone and your voice. It's also a way to differentiate yourself. It's an extension of you. It helps you connect with others and engage in more authentic and natural ways. It's your reputation.

You don't have to be an online celebrity to have a Personal Brand. In fact, you're already cultivating your brand by the choices you make. What you wear, how you speak, what you like to listen to and read. And of course your Digital Footprint.

It's not a question of if, rather when.
If you don't take responsibility for the way you are portrayed online as well as
offline,
it will find its own default setting.

Whether you just show the highlight reel on social media or go all out with the good, the bad and the ugly, that's up to you. Your Digital Footprint is there for all to see. You may as well guide and cultivate it consciously.

Branding is an evolution. Just as you grow and evolve, so too does your Personal Brand. Make a start and build from where you are now. It's an exciting journey that will help you confidently stand out and be authentically yourself. Think about your personality for a moment. A great barometer of what you're about, your Personal Brand communicates your strengths and your uniqueness. Everything you do should feel right and be aligned or in tune with your values and the things you stand for.

Your Personal Brand, your way

Your values can be any number of things you choose, like honesty, belonging, connection, bravery, confidence, family, friends, knowledge, playfulness or trust. The list is endless. The important part to keep in mind is that the values you choose should be meaningful to you and feel good to *you*. They are what you stand for.

All great brands have clearly defined values (just like you will), which Monika then gets to know and study. She will revisit a brand's values exercise before she starts working on a campaign. She identifies what the product or service holds important, the principles it stands for. For Monika, she has what you might like to call a friendship checklist. All the things that are important for her that she likes to tick off before she shares them with friends who have similar values.

You don't necessarily *tell* people what your values are. They just know. It's the way you are and how you behave. A great example of a Personal Brand communicating its values is Taylor Swift. One of her values, supporting the underdog and smaller artists, was demonstrated when she challenged iTunes over not paying artists while their customers were on their free three-month trial. Bold, right? Taylor withdrew her album at the time and Apple responded by agreeing to pay all artists for their work, even during the time they ran the free trial promotion. She didn't *tell* people what was important. She *showed* them.

Now it's time to take a closer look at a Personal Brand that has your name all over it. *Your* Personal Brand.

your exclusive personal brand

Let's find out what's important to you, what makes you tick, your 'core values'. Your values are the principles you feel strongly about, what you're passionate about, your standards on what's important in life. These core values will shape your Personal Brand.

When you're clear on your values, it's easier to make decisions. You have your values to guide you. Your values are a map for *you*. What makes you happy and feel good about yourself. So let's explore this map a little more.

♥ List three brands that you love. (These can be global brands or local to your community.)

♥ Why do you love these brands? List three reasons for each one.

♥ How do each of these brands make you feel when you see/think of them?

♥ What kind of brands do you not like?

♥ What is it about these brands that you don't like?

Keeping in mind your answers above, choose 10 words to capture your own values (or choose from the sample list below). These values will reflect what you perceive as important in the world.

Sample Values List

Achievement, Altruism, Ambition, Assertiveness, Balance, Belonging, Boldness, Calm, Challenge, Community, Contentment, Creativity, Determination, Diversity, Equality, Empathy, Expressiveness, Focus, Fun, Freedom, Growth, Generosity, Honesty, Happiness, Health, Intuition, Inquisitiveness, Love, Leadership, Loyalty, Legacy, Making a Difference, Openness, Peace, Positivity, Resourcefulness, Security, Service, Simplicity, Strength, Sensitivity, Trust, Teamwork, Understanding, Vision

10 words to describe your exclusive Personal Brand:

1.

2.

3.

4.

5.

6.

7.

8.

9.

10.

Emotional branding and emotional connection

How does Monika make you feel? A big question which can have many different answers, depending on when Monika is talking to you. In Monika's world, she uses these feelings to move you to take action or buy something. Feelings are powerful and useful in Monika's world. When Monika's message speaks directly to your feelings, it makes it seem like she's talking directly to you, right?

Other times you might see an ad and the images have very little to do with the product. A soft drink ad, for example, might have lots of fun images of young people doing activities that make us feel good. Coca-Cola does this exceptionally well. In Australia, you might have seen the Subway ad with friends surfing, active and laughing at the beach with friends, eating Subway.

These images (*not the product itself*) make us feel good. Then when we see the brand mentioned in the ad, we subconsciously associate the brand with these emotions. This is called 'emotional branding'. Regardless of how realistic it is, the brand has successfully achieved its purpose of association. We feel happy when we see the ad and associate the brand with these feelings. This leads us to talking about how we buy.

Feel now, think later

We buy stuff and make purchase decisions on emotion, not logic. That's why Monika taps directly into emotions first. Your feelings are a big part of what she does next. Feelings of seeking, belonging and acceptance are normal for everyone.

Fear is also another popular one. You might be moved to do something because you are afraid of the consequences if you don't. For example, you go to the movies with your friends, even though you don't like the horror movie that's showing. You're afraid you'll miss out on something if you don't go!

Trendsetting is also popular with Monika and her mob. You see celebrities, actors and sporting champions promote products. This positions and places the brand as 'cool and trendy' and by default you can become cool and trendy when you use the product too.

These strategies or smart little plans aren't all bad news. They can be used for good too. The reason it's good for you to be aware of them is to understand why you feel and act a certain way, after seeing marketing and advertising messages. We talked a lot about awareness in the first chapter and then elaborated on your personal values and brand in this chapter. Remember your personal values, your standards, what you believe in and what you love? Remember using these as your decision-guiding principles? Well, now is the time you come back to these values.

When you feel emotionally triggered, it's because you identify with what's in Monika's message. It is speaking directly to you. That's not to say your feelings are wrong. It's more about being aware of the feeling and managing it in the best way for you.

What you like versus what Monika likes

Looking at your answers from your Personal Brand Playsheet, do you think Monika would agree with your values and standards for yourself? Do you think that matters? Of course not. Monika is just a voice, a face to a product or brand. Another opinion. She's not you.

Monika likes to encourage you to look outside of yourself for comfort, acceptance and direction. When you do that, you are more likely to agree with her and behave the way she would like you to behave. Can you see, by looking to Monika for approval, you lose the ability to listen to your own thoughts and recognise your own inner compass?

Monika will always promise you something better. That's just the way she is. By nature, Monika and her marketing buddies are always offering solutions. Solutions to problems you may not even have!

Offering products and services to 'improve' your life in some way. You'll be tempted to become more beautiful or popular, have better self-confidence, friendships and relationships - you name it - even when you don't need to make improvements and changes in these areas of your life.

But in order for you to even consider these 'offers' and how best to deal with them through the media, you must have a reference point. That reference point is you and your values. The answers you give yourself first.

Taking time out from Monika and saying no!

There are times when you really don't need more *stuff.* There are times when maybe you're not sure and don't know if you need more stuff. There are times when you just *want* more stuff. It keeps you busy, distracted. Then there are times you don't want to have to make any more decisions. There are times when you simply want some peace and quiet.

For all of these occasions, you need a handy Do I or Don't I? Checklist, to guide you towards the next step. Here it is.

do I or don't I? checklist

10 questions to ask yourself before you commit to buying (or doing) anything:

1. Do I really want this or does Monika want it for me?

2. Can I wait a few days and see how I feel about it then?

3. Is this item or image trying to make me someone I'm not?

4. Is saying yes making me feel more in control? If so, why?

5. Am I speaking up and using my own voice in this decision?

6. Am I buying this to fit in because all my friends have it?

7. What's the worst thing that could happen if I *don't* buy or do it?

8. Is that 'worst thing that could happen' really that bad?

9. What could I choose to focus on or spend my money on instead?

10. What would the 'good enough' me do, the girl who doesn't care what other people think?

By going through these questions, you get to stay aware and in control. You're asking yourself for answers that you have within you, *before* listening to advice from Monika and her marketing mob. It empowers *you* to make the decisions, not her. You get to decide. Awesome, right?

Of course, there are times like birthdays and other celebrations and special occasions in life where you want to spend your money. Deservedly! There may simply be essentials that you really do need. This Do I or Don't I? Checklist is not for those occasions. It's to help you manage daily challenges and distractions for what Monika calls *must-haves*, which you see repeatedly and that trigger you.

Unique and different is the new generation of beautiful... You don't have to be like everyone else.
In fact, I don't think you should.
~ Taylor Swift

Respect yo'self and flex some self-love muscle

What does self-respect look like for you? Self-respect for me is being proud of my actions, considerate of my true feelings, looking after how I treat my body and staying true to myself.

Achieving this is no easy task. And it isn't a recipe for a perfectly packaged you either. You can do all this and still be really hard on yourself. That part I know from experience! Being hard on yourself looks like judging yourself, not feeling good enough, beating yourself up that you could have done better. Always more, more, more to do. Recognise any of those feelings?

That kind of chasing is exhausting, let me tell you. It's not the healthy striving that champions are made of. It's the struggle of self-sabotage that leads most commonly to disappointment. And Monika and her marketing peeps can spot that a mile away. In fact, they thrive on it.

If that sounds familiar to you, perhaps you're missing out on a good dose of self-love. Now before your eyes glaze over and you think this is all way too deep or woowoo, wait up! Don't lose me here. I'm not going to launch into a book on self-love. I'm still figuring that out for myself for heaven's sake! There are many amazing resources out there that explain and encourage it beautifully. Check out the further resources at the back of this book for some radical self-love suggestions and put an end to those chattering 'I'm not good enough' voices.

Let me ask you, on any given day, how many of the following five words would you associate with how you speak to yourself?

Kindness
Compassion
Consideration
Forgiveness
Understanding

So how many out of five did you score? If you're lower than two then it's time for some self-love, my dear. Think about it another way. Would you speak to your best friend the way you speak to yourself on a regular basis? If the answer is a resounding '*no!*' then you deserve better.

You are better than this. Monika and the marketing gang will drive you completely nuts if she knows you speak to yourself without kindness, without forgiveness. She will cause you to question yourself and lose every ounce of confidence to back your own opinions and choices. Not good.

Being you is not some exam that you pass or fail. This is not a test. This is a journey we're all on. And we are doing the best we can. Including you. Building up your self-love muscles not only helps you become the best version of you, but it also means when Monika and her marketing peeps are way too noisy, making you feel insecure, doubtful or inadequate, you are in a much healthier place to resist these distractions. Self-love is your very own built-in protection system.

In a society that profits from your self-doubt and insecurities,
this inner compass is a valuable asset to have.

Great work on creating your Personal Brand and unique core values! Don't forget to refer back to you Do I or Don't I? Checklist anytime you have a big purchase decision to make. We squeezed in a few extra activities in this chapter, compared to what's coming in the following ones, so well done for sticking with it.

These supreme skills will come in handy for the upcoming stages in your friendship with Monika. Next up, we'll be finding out exactly where Monika hangs out. And more importantly, when she likes to pop up and surprise you!

If you haven't already, don't forget to check out your extra resources and downloadable goodies at www.helenroe.com/girltribes (You can thank me later. ☺)

Chapter 3

Where Monika Hangs Out

Home is where your story begins.

You're a loser. You're so uncool. Excuse me? How rude is that? I know! Sorry to break it to you, but that's exactly the message a lot of advertising is indirectly portraying. Corporations and big brands tend to capitalise on your insecurities and self-doubts, encouraging you to believe that to be accepted and cool you need their product.

Of course, you probably knew that. Or maybe you think they are talking to someone else? You feel you're not part of that club. But you're actually in it, right where they want you to be. Unsure, inquisitive and ready to learn more.

Don't get me wrong, these feelings are quite normal. What's not OK is when you feel this unsure, inquisitive and ready to learn, then Monika (AKA that ever-present marketing mob again) goes and puts a picture of perfection in front of you. It can make you feel 10 times worse. *Oh hey there, Monika!* Deep down, you know those models in that ad don't reflect real life. It's just a matter of remembering to question it. Do *all* the girls in *your* class look like that? Ask yourself that question next time you see an ad pop up.

♥ In this chapter, we are going to learn how Monika is so clever and smart, and somehow manages to be everyone's friend without much effort. You'll understand why people like her have certain personality traits to watch for. And you'll get to see behind the scenes of where she hangs out. (Hint: it's not just in the obvious places you might think.)

So why you?

Great question. Surely big brands and corporations would be better advertising to adults with real incomes and more money to spend? Well, they do that too. However, you are part of a lucrative empire called the Teen Market. This market influences hundreds of billions of dollars' worth of spending. Bet you didn't realise just how much buying power and influence you really had, did you? Marketers, Monika and big brands want a piece of that pie.

Some companies actually have 'cool hunters' who literally hunt out what's cool amongst teens. (Try suggesting that job description next time you're talking with your career officer!) These cool hunters then bring back their latest market research and use these findings to tailor their marketing campaigns. They tell Monika what to say and how to dress, so she fits right in. Monika is their vehicle or messenger and she knows a lot more about you than you realise.

Sometimes the company behind Monika is offering a solution to your needs. Sometimes it's creating a problem, which in turn creates a need for a solution, so that company can step in and offer the solution, their product or service. A little confusing, I agree. It's unfair to generalise and paint every brand with the same brush, of course. That' why it's so important for you to be able to make a judgement call yourself.

Move Over Monika

Some brands market to your insecurities and your-self-doubt. Can you recall a brand or particular advertisement where this happened?

Challenge what you see in the media with your friends. Spark a conversation about the worst ad you've seen. Or even the best. Get some feedback and share it using the hashtag #GirlTribes. I'd love to hear what your detective work uncovers!

Advertising and body image

Monika is everywhere for good reason. When she's associated with brands, she sells stuff. Whether you like how she looks or not, her 'perfect' flawless face, her pearly white smile and her fit, toned and tanned body is what makes people take notice. Even if you're not buying, but just flipping through a magazine or socialising online, the obsession with looks is everywhere. In particular, the 'before and after' seems a real winner.

I'm all for self-improvement and keeping fit and healthy. There's always room to learn in this department, right? But it can be hard to develop a healthy love for yourself and your body when the media is portraying perfection as the norm. Who really looks like that? (Only Monika of course). These images of thin, beautiful, sexualised girls are mainstream stereotypes of success and happiness. They do not represent the majority of the population. Yet because of the power of advertising and its pervasiveness – Monika is everywhere, remember – this message can reach far and wide.

Where does that leave the majority of us, the rest of the female population? Comparison, insecurity, self-doubt, preoccupation with our looks and trying to *fit in* are just some of the side effects from the continuous drip feed of the media's obsession with women's looks. How can we feel good about ourselves if we are constantly comparing our looks to some unrealistic (in fact, completely fake) idea of perfection?

The stereotypes of girls portrayed in the majority of media messages look something like this: girls are fragile, pretty fashionistas, fixated with boys, obsessed with their bodies, always shopping with friends and looking up to celebrities. On the other hand, boys are strong, independent, sporty types, into online gaming, adventure, music and hanging with their friends. And those are not my words. These come straight from a survey I did of over 100 teen girls. Here's some more insights into what teen girls like you have shared with me about how they feel after seeing girls in media advertising.

'It seems every girl should look the way girls do on TV. To be happy, you need to have a great body. I feel very self-conscious about how skinny I am and if my hair is good enough. I feel jealous and want to do the all of the things they do. I was looking at girls on the internet who were my age and suddenly thought I was fat (even though I'm not). I felt really self-conscious for about two years and at one point didn't want to eat anything for a while. I am always questioning myself if I look good enough and if my friends will be impressed by me.'
~ *Alison, fourteen*

'When I see advertisements with girls my age in them it makes me feel sad and angry because they are misinterpreting girls our age and think of us as older teenagers, i.e. we should be wearing inappropriate clothes and are always on social media.'
~ *Maria, twelve*

They say comparison is the thief of joy and yes there is a bucket load of research to back this up. But it's also worth mentioning, we are hardwired for comparison. Huh? But isn't that the thief of your joy? Let me explain. Using a story about monkeys...

Two monkeys are trained to exchange small stones in return for some cucumber. The monkeys are happy with this arrangement until one of the monkeys is given a sweet grape instead of a cucumber. (A bit like humans, monkeys prefer something sweet). When the other monkey saw he was getting a lesser deal, he went a little crazy. He started throwing the cucumber back at the experimenter's face, refusing to play the exchange game and even shaking the screen in anger. It's fascinating to watch and hilarious. You can see this famous experiment in action in footage on the TEDx talk by the scientist Frans De Waal. Just Google it and watch to the end.

This experiment may be a long way from the shiny glowing images in your Instagram feed, but it comes down to the same behaviour. What it shows is that even our evolutionary ancestors, the monkeys, do not evaluate and measure their situation on their own or in isolation. They compare and see how others are doing to learn more about themselves.

So if comparison is in evitable and helps us make sense of our world, how can we use comparison in a positive way? Depending on how you look at it, comparison can make you miserable or it can motivate you. 'She's gorgeous. I will never look that good.' That type of comparison equals misery. 'She's awesome. I can feel that happy and confident too.' That type of approach creates motivation to improve and challenge yourself.

#selfies go pro and get #fitspo

Ah yes, the legendary selfie. As a somewhat retired youth, I didn't grow up with smartphones held in outstretched arms populating my vision. I have my eyes closed in most of my childhood pics! I've had a camera aversion from a young age. I'm recovering, but still adjusting, so if you have any tips, do let me know. I hear holding the camera at eye level or below is a no-no?

I do think the selfie culture is a great platform for creative self-expression. You are the photographer and you get to have fun with it. Plus it's empowering. And that's all great. But it's also where Monika makes a big impact, so let's talk about 'professional' selfies in Monika's world. Some of these dewy-faced glorified #selfies captured on Instagram feeds are now a lucrative (#cash) platform for Monika, her marketers and indeed the 'sponsored' Lycra-clad participants.

There's nothing new with bloggers getting paid for their work. But health, fitness and clean-eating interspersed with motivational quotes and 'cheat days', all while looking good in Lycra, has never been so popular. Or so profitable. Welcome to the world of #fitspo and sponsored content.

I do believe the majority of Instagram stars are well-intentioned and, as I'm sure you do, I totally support self- improvement and being the best version of ourselves. The waters get a little murky when it's not all as it seems. In other words, the reality of a person's life is nothing like their online Instagram feed. Yes, we all enjoy seeing the highlight reel, the best bits. No-one wants to see doom and gloom, broken toe-nails and bad hair days. But when is online gloss going too far?

I am always am questioning myself if I look good enough and if my friends will be impressed by me.'
~ *Rachel, thirteen*

'I automatically compare myself. I end up feeling down and not good enough.'
~ *Suzi, sixteen*

'When I see girls online and in ads it makes me feel left out, a bit down, and I wish I was like them.'
~ *Jacinta, fourteen*

Influencers and online 'experts'

Social media is a tool. Like everything Monika is involved in, it can be of value and help people. Then again, it can be just the opposite. You, the user, have a responsibility to use it wisely. It's easy to sit and agree to that, but we all know how addictive social media scrolling can get. So what can you do?

To start off with, set some simple boundaries. Be selective with what you watch and who you follow. Do they align with your values and your beliefs? Next, surround yourself with people who make you feel great about yourself and support you when you're feeling down. Remember, influencers or Insta 'experts' are not health experts. A lip-smacking smoothie and a bowl of granola (gluten-free, of course) does not an expert make. Unfortunately, Monika is not the best at practicing this. As one of the online influencers, she gets paid in sponsored posts to behave a certain way, wear a certain thing, use a certain product and give a certain endorsement. She certainly shows the highlights, the best bits.

Think of it like this. When you pass a beautiful house with a gorgeous garden bursting with colour, you don't automatically think, '*Wow! The person who lives in there must be soooo happy!*' Sure, you can imagine and wonder who lives there, but really you've no clue about them as a person. They could be renting the space or terminally ill. You don't know what's going on behind closed doors. Same goes for IG pics. Glowing feeds curated with pristine images are not the full story. Take it for what it is. A photo (likely retouched), not a life story.

I enjoy following inspirational accounts that share ideas I love – whole food, yoga and fitness, natural products and more. I'm not suggesting that everything body image or food-related is bad. It's simply not always the full picture. Everything is relative. Be discerning. Stay curious and question if you're OK with sponsorship in your feed. Is the brand aligned with your values and real life priorities? Does it entertain, educate or help you feel good about yourself? If not, then it's time to reconsider why you follow that brand.

Speaking of real life, The Body Image Movement based in Australia is a global movement calling girls and women to embrace the skin they're in. Promoting body loving over body loathing, Taryn Brumfitt's Body Image Movement is inspiring women all around the world to love and accept their bodies. I saw Taryn speak at a conference in Adelaide and she had the audience (including me!) in tears. I was a speaker at the event too and was up straight after Taryn (no pressure then). I had just shed tears of solidarity with a room full of women and the next minute was landed the challenge of exciting this same audience on the scintillating topic of sales and marketing. I can safely say, if you were in the audience, it was a good time to nip out for a toilet break. But on a more body-positive note, if you'd like to learn how you can join the Embrace movement, check out www.bodyimagemovement.com

Maybe you've also heard of the #freshfacedfriday Tear It Up campaign in Australia? It's about ensuring positive self-talk gets more airtime than negative. When we feel good about ourselves and our body, it has awesome knock-on effects in other areas of our life such as our relationships, self-esteem and confidence.

Move Over Monika

How can you further develop your healthy body image? Perhaps focus less on body size and shape, but more on sending nice messages to yourself in your head, which is called positive self-talk. Be mindful of what you watch, what you post, who you follow etc. Does the media you consume support you in feeling good about yourself? Choose to follow positive role models who represent a healthy attitude to body image and self-esteem. (Hint: that's not just models).

Staying aware that what we see in the media online, in print and on TV is often manipulated will help you challenge the messages you're exposed to. Even if this is simply a conversation you have with your friend, it will help reduce the possible negative impact it can have on you.

Hello Monika!

So now you're more aware of how Monika shows up and the way she might make you feel, what can you do? You've no doubt tried to ignore media marketing, dismissed it or maybe even ridiculed it. That's on a good day.

What about the days where you're just having one of *those* days? What about when that picture of the slim, sexy and oh-so-cool girl promoting [insert any must-have product that you have your eyes on]

makes everything feel better? That's the time you need to *really* keep vigilant about what you let yourself watch, read and listen to. We all love a little comfort on our off-days. In marketing terms, that's Monika.

Monika will always be quick to notice your vulnerable days. She's been working hard to be aware of it. She wants to help, of course, but sometimes what she thinks is the solution usually isn't at all what you need. Maybe you don't *need* anything. Maybe you need someone to listen, rather than yet more advice or problem-fixing.

When you're feeling curious, confused, insecure, upset or lonely, listening to Monika's It-Girl opinions might make you feel better. Briefly. After all, she's happy, beautiful and seems to have everything going for her, right? Except for one thing. Monika. Is. Not. Real. She's acting. She's simply doing her job. She's got her best smile on for the camera and for you. She's being paid quite a lot to say and do exactly what she is told.

When Monika triggers you

So what can you do when you know you're having a weak moment, an off-day or simply want to ignore Monika effectively? Well, the great thing is you *do* have a choice. Like I said before, you get to be in control and make the decision here. Grab your Save The Day Playsheet in your free Action Kit on the website at www.helenroe.com/girltribes for an instant mood-booster when Monika triggers you.

When Monika gets sneaky

Yes, she does that sometimes. She gets a little pushy, and before you know you it, you've agreed to whatever it is she's rambling on about. Just to get some peace and quiet. And maybe because you don't want to seem rude or feel you might miss out on something. All perfectly normal. And she knows that.

Here are some of the ways you might see Monika sneaking up on you. Stay aware, stay curious and you'll be just fine.

Vouchers and coupons

Sure, that $10 off your next purchase for dog food or toilet roll is super handy. Things you actually need. $10 off your next purchase at Gap or your favourite online retailer just encourages you to want to spend, though, right? And who doesn't love a discount? But did you really need to buy that extra item in the first place?

Time is running out!

Also referred to as 'time-sensitive' marketing, this is when a discount or bonus offer ends by a certain date. Usually when you check, it'll be in just 24 to 48 hours. And there are only a few left in your size or your favourite colour. It's just so tempting. There's something about having an offer that's only around for a short time to make us buy. If we're lucky on the timing, it can work in our favour. Other times we end up buying on impulse, rushing into a purchase and regretting it later. Monika is there saying 'hurry up, it will be gone if you don't grab it now' and it's just so hard to resist sometimes. Yep, we all feel this one creep up occasionally.

Free gift with purchase

This is a popular one around key calendar dates through the year like Christmas, Valentines and Easter. When you buy a certain item, you get a free gift. Yay! Sometimes the gifts are really cool too. I often wait to buy my personal care top-ups when my favourite brand is offering their super cute bonus wash bag and travel minis with purchase. Nothing dodgy about that at all. Except... when you buy the product purely to get the free item. Uh-oh! You've fallen foul to Monika's marketing ways.

Buy-one-get-one-free

These offers always seems great at first, don't they? I mean who doesn't want a free shower gel or toothpaste or choccy bar? Actually you. You do not need two. And if you're buying your twin pack to store the spare one and stock up, good for you. You are one of the very few. The rest of us? We contribute to the practice of expandable consumption – the more we buy, the more we use.

That shower gel twin pack with one bottle free? We lather that stuff all over us in the shower. Oops – just spilt a bit there! If it's Tim Tams, we eat 'just one more' to round it off. And if it's deodorant, we spray that stuff so furiously you could see it in space. You get the idea. Free stuff doesn't always mean we put it aside so we don't have to buy it next week.

Targeted online advertising

You probably know about cookies – those little trawlers on your laptop and phone. Monika and her crew love the insights these little fellas provide. They almost sound cute. Ha! Smart cookies, indeed. They tell Monika's team what site you were browsing, what shoe style you clicked on, what brand you like. It's no coincidence that an ad for that *very* top you were looking at yesterday just popped into the sidebar on your Facebook feed. It's tailored and served up especially for you.

Maybe you bought something online and the store is popping into your feed to remind you to come visit the latest stock arrival. Awesome! How nice of them! ☺ (Note to self: I do not have to click on every distraction presented to me, no matter how gorgeous it looks!)

Impulse buys at the checkout

These are the items you see at the checkout while waiting to pay. They're usually smaller items, sweets or candy, and other low-price-point products. In some countries, it's now illegal in supermarkets to sell chocolate and tempting sweets at the checkouts. Think: frustrated impatient child screaming because they can't have the chocolate. It's been a long day. Mum gives in.

For you, if you're in a department store, you might see sunnies, nail care products, hair accessories, travel items and other small temptations while you stand in line. When you buy these items, it's called an impulse purchase. You never planned to buy them and you do so very quickly without much thought. You act on impulse.

Shake it to the right

Oh yes, your savvy friend Monika is very much into grooving to the right side of the store. Her marketing team and their studies have revealed we shop best moving from the right to the left, walking counter-clockwise around a store.

Some clothes stores seem very much a mess though, don't they? Certainly there isn't always the right to left movement happening. You saunter in and suddenly you're in the thick of it. Turns here, displays there, sale racks wherever. Lots of stimulation and distraction; so much so you nearly forget what you came in for! Marketing mission accomplished. You browse longer and have a greater chance of buying more. (Yay, this will cheer Monika up).

Fresh and mmm-mmm

I'm sure you've often noticed the aroma of fresh bread emanating from the grocery store. There's good reason to write your list *before* you go shopping. Or maybe the cheery fragrant fresh flowers right at the entrance? Or a high impact display as you enter the department store that encourages you to slow down and perhaps touch, smell or taste? Activating the senses is great for marketers trying to encourage you to make impulse purchases.

I love flowers at the entrance to the supermarket. They put a smile on my face! Tick, Monika has offered me a warm welcome. First impressions count, so Monika makes sure what you see, smell and taste first is something you're going to love! Anyway, you'll need to keep your spirits high as you trek to the very back of the store to buy your essentials, like milk and butter, passing all the temptation along the way, of course!

I've got you in my sights

Monika has so many great products she wants to share with you. But she knows realistically you can't buy them all. (She's good like that). However, she does like to help you make your decision. In Monika's world this is called space management where category managers and their teams use sophisticated software to design layouts of shelves and where each brand will sit on the shelf. It's all about maximising sales and the customer experience (i.e. making it enjoyable and easy to find what they're looking for).

When you're in the supermarket, she will ensure you see the best-selling brands first. These are the higher priced branded goods and they sit about midway up the shelves at eye-level. She's even thought of the little ones and has their favourite treats and snacks at *their* eye level too! ☺ You'll also catch popular items and items on promotion on display again, at the end of aisles, just in case you miss them. This is also prime real estate that a brand pays a lot for the benefit of being there.

Pretty colours

You probably know that certain colours evoke specific feelings and emotions. It's fascinating, isn't it? Colour psychology is simply the study of colour and how it affects human behaviour. Monika uses colour in marketing all the time. Colour helps Monika and her marketing team portray her message and get you to see what she wants you to see, feel what she wants you to feel and do what she wants you to do.

Colours can make certain spaces look so inviting. Often, we see calming colours like white, pale blue and mint green in bedrooms. That's because they invoke a sense of peace and serenity. It works the same way when companies advertise products and services. You might see stronger colours like red and blue, making a product stand out, loud and clear.

Here's a quick guide to colour emotions that outlines the more popular colours and the emotions they evoke.

White/Grey	Balance, Calm, Peace
Green	Growth, Health
Blue	Trust, Dependability, Strength
Purple	Creativity, Imagination, Wisdom
Red	Excitement, Youth, Boldness
Orange	Friendliness, Cheerfulness, Confidence
Yellow	Warmth, Happiness, Optimism
Black	Power, Elegance, Formality

Music, mirrors and lighting

Music, as you know, creates atmosphere. Great music in your favourite clothes shop keeps your energy high and makes your shopping experience fun. Studies show that loud music makes shoppers move quickly and make faster decisions. In supermarkets, slower music is often played to prolong cruising the aisles and encouraging you to fill your trolley.

We've all been there. Tried something on in the store changing room and it looked like it was made for you. Get it home and it resembles something closer to a sack. Fitting room mirrors can be tilted ever so slightly upwards to flatter and elongate the body. Soft lighting creates a flattering halo effect, making you look a size smaller as well as an angel come down from heaven. The opposite can often happen too. Harsh direct lighting makes lumps and bumps appear from nowhere!

Loyalty cards

I'm sure you have more than one of these in your wallet. I know I do! It can be a love-hate relationship. It's great to get rewards and discounts for shopping in your favourite store. And when they send you birthday wishes (along with a voucher or coupon), you feel special. But sometimes it gets annoying with all the emails and reminders. Spend $50 and get $10 off. Have you ever spent more than you intended, just to receive the $10 off? Me too.

This loyalty card keeps you loyal to the brand, while offering the business you're buying from a wealth of information and tracking about your preferences and spending habits.

And what about this?

I'm sure you've seen this when you've been shopping for clothes. Beside the dresses or tops, you'll see some complementary scarves, belts or bags. Each item goes beautifully with what's beside it, to complete the look. Tempting and super convenient too. This is genius. Even though I'm aware of the strategy, I *still* buy into sometimes! (After I've run through my Do I or Don't I? Checklist first, of course.)

Similarly, you may find when you're buying online, you'll see the lovely reminders 'you might also like this' or 'shoppers also bought'. This is what we call cross-selling. It encourages the shopper – that's you, by the way – to ultimately buy more. Another version of this is when you're trying on a top and the shop assistant offers some recommendations of more expensive styles, which might 'suit you better'. This is upselling. You are encouraged to buy 'up' in price and for a better product.

What was I thinking?'

We've all been there. You buy something because it seems like a fantastic idea at the time. Only later do you realise it was terrible mistake and you regret your purchase. It's not possible to return the item because, in your excitement, you a) cut the tags off or b) threw out the receipt. You are experiencing buyer's remorse – that sinking feeling when you hand over the cash, leave the store and hear that annoying voice telling you *'you shouldn't have bought that'* or *'what were you thinking?'* Regret is written all over your face. It's no fun and can make us feel silly, stupid and so frustrated with ourselves.

Some of Monika's moves above, including impulse buying, can result in you buying items you later regret and big-time buyer's remorse. It can often be heightened by the anticlimax after the fun shopping experience. What goes up must come down, right? Now you just have an ill-fitting outfit and an empty wallet.

To avoid feeling remorse in the first place, it helps to know why you want to buy something. If it's something you want because all your friends are buying it, then beware. Alarm bells are ringing! Feeling pressure to buy is never a good reason to buy anything.

'When I was younger, I thought it was cool to have the same stationery (Smiggle) as my friends and thought they wouldn't accept me unless I had such stationery. It didn't really work out because by the time I did have the stationery, a new trend had set in!'
~ *Mandy, twelve*

Some simple steps you can take to avoid buyer's remorse include checking the stores returns policy before you purchase. Watch for Monika's pushy panicky tactics that we talked about earlier, such as invitations to *act now* and that something will only be available for a *limited time*. And get familiar with asking yourself the Do I or Don't I? Checklist from chapter 2 before you make a big decision.

Rainbows and unicorns or real life?

I'm sure you've noticed at this stage that Monika is always perfect. She never seems to have a bad hair day. Marketing and the media, her crowd, are always on their game. They always look together and it all looks effortless. Monika lives in a rainbows-and-unicorns world. It's pretty. But it isn't real.

Rainbows are beautiful and we see them from time to time. Unicorns, although magical, are imaginary mythical creatures. What you see in advertisements online and in magazines is a bit like that. It's nice to visit there once in a while, but it's not real everyday life.

When we see this idyllic perfect world in the media, it can easily start to feel like the norm. If we see something often enough, we start to take notice and the message can make a visible impact. We can even be persuaded into thinking this message is correct or the only answer, the best solution or the next must-have.

If you are always trying to fit into a perceived 'normal',
you will never discover how incredibly wonderful you truly are.

What exactly is perfection anyway? Is it some idea we have about the way things should be? Or perhaps how people should look or behave? Spoiler alert. Perfection in everyday life is non-existent. It's a myth and it's not real. What's real is showing up as you – brave, scared, excited, bored, making mistakes, saying sorry, crying, laughing, learning, growing and living. It's a rollercoaster ride. It's a mixed bag. It's a kaleidoscope of colours, including the ones you don't like.

Life does not require perfection

Life requires you to be you and show up as you. By that I mean being honest and true to yourself and your values, doing things that support your Personal Brand. (You can always recap on your values back in chapter 2.) Saying yes when you feel it's a yes. Saying no when you feel it's a no. Asking for help and advice when you're unsure. Or when you simply want someone to listen.

Since you have years ahead of you to figure this out, this isn't something you have to decide right now. It's an evolving process. We don't just pop out of the box ready-made, perfect and all together, as the finished product. It's a journey. We grow and learn on that journey. Trying this, checking out that, exploring and discovering. All part of your incredible journey.

I make mistakes growing up. I'm not perfect, I'm not a robot.
~ Justin Bieber

It's an exciting time, exploring life as a teen girl. That's why Monika and the marketing mob like to influence you. Because they can. You're receptive and open to new experiences. Monika has lots to share with you and it's fun times ahead. Don't worry though. This is a game for two! You will be just as prepared as Monika and understand the best choices to make, what to do and when.

Don't forget to go to www.helenroe.com/girltribes for your free Action Kit packed with extra goodies to support you your media-savvy self.

Please share your stories, your ups and your downs with the #GirlTribes hashtag. I'm excited to hear from you and learn how you're getting on with your new friend Monika! This marketing girl has met her match. You're getting clued-up and ready to make your mark.

Next up, we will delve further into the world of InstaCelebs and influencers online, how they help Monika and how you are part of the process, without even realising it.

Chapter 4

The Secrets of Influencers
and #InstaCelebs

What have you done today to make you feel proud? It's never too late to try.
We need a change. Do it today.
~ Heather Small

You. Have. The. Power. *Yes, you!* You and only you get to control how you feel and the choices you make. Simple really. Monika and her like-minded marketing influencers will try to dominate that power. Initially, it might look like sharing, but ultimately much of their influence will attempt to dominate your decision-making. Your job is to hold on to that power. Real tight. Monika is always there to offer you her advice and recommendations. Remember how she always seems to have the solution? Well, her parents (AKA the marketing department) have her well-versed on what to say to you and when to say it.

♥ In this chapter, we take a look at Monika and her team of influencers. Who are these #InstaCelebs and online influencers? How do they persuade you and win you over to their way of thinking? We look at some of Monika's superpowers, her propaganda techniques and who she calls on for back-up support. You're sure to recognise a few! Read on.

I'm not saying don't listen to Monika ever! Of course there are times when you see an ad or a recommendation for a great product that just fits, seems right and offers some kind of solution. Whether that's to entertain, education or ease your mind, it doesn't matter.

What matters is that you feel confident and strong enough to say no when you need to. Whether that's when you're on your own, with your friends or when things aren't going well. There will be times when you are more vulnerable to what Monika has to say. It will persuade you. Let's be sure it's for the right reasons.

Your choice starts first with awareness. When I say awareness, I don't mean just seeing or hearing an ad and observing 'oh yeah, that ad is trying to persuade me' type of awareness. I mean real deep down honest understanding about what's being *triggered* in you. The psychology behind the ad or the marketing message Monika is delivering. Yep, going deeper here. Not quite to the level of a degree in psychology; just looking at the thinking behind the actions a little more. Why Monika does what she does.

Monika's role is one of an influencer. She loves to invite you into her tribe and make you a part of her valued community. I'm sure you know people like this. Sometimes Monika leads and influences in a good way. Others times it's a no-no. It's useful to know how to identify both.

Not 100% sure? I understand. It can be tricky when you're used to taking Monika at face value. It's important to question, '*Really - can you make me look that good, just by wearing that top?*' Follow these steps to help you decide. Carefully assess and review Monika's invitation. See if it's relevant and worthwhile for you. Choose accordingly. Do you want to be part of that online conversation? Does the product make you feel better in some way? Do the brand values align with your own personal values and what's important to you? Answer these questions first, then have the conversation with Monika.

#InstaCelebs and high-profile influencers

Monika appears through the media in many disguises. Sometimes she's just a regular girl next door. Other times she's in the form of a well-known celebrity, singer, YouTube sensation, InstaCeleb. You know how it works.

Influencers of any kind help Monika's boss (that's the big brands and businesses she works for) to reach more people, grow awareness for their brand and generate more profit. Yes, it's a worthwhile Monika move. Do you follow any influencers online? If so, what do you love about them and why? Influencers also help transport you to cultures and other parts of the globe that we otherwise wouldn't have access to. A behind-the-scenes with Michelle Obama at the White House. Scroll away. Beyoncé releases video clips of her new single. Awesome. A day in the life of [insert your fave celebrity] and away you go.

When Monika partners with social media influencers (those with zillions of followers), it's showcase time. These online 'celebrities' endorse products, usually in return for payment, and the brands receive massive exposure to new audiences. It can increase the brand's credibility and reputation instantly. You, the follower, will trust the brand more too, when you see someone you admire using a particular product. It also positions the product in its best light, demonstrating who the product is for. Clever, huh?

These influencers are trusted by their loyal followers for their opinions, habits, lifestyles, and in many cases are experts in their field. Partnering with influencers is popular on Instagram right now, because of the visual aspect. Beautiful photography makes the products look appealing. And it's more than just a brochure. It's a lifestyle perspective. You get to actually see the person using said product in their life. You may have seen examples of this with clothes and fashion, food, health and wellness, beauty and more. Product endorsements or product placements are commonly used for promotions, giveaways and launches.

Kayla Itsines is an example in Australia of a successful social media influencer. The fitness trainer has amassed a following of 4.9 million promoting her Bikini Body Guide, training videos and the ever-so-popular before and after photos of her clients. *Time* has declared her one of the most influential people on the internet!

When Monika uses influencers, she puts her trust in another person (online personality, celebrity, call it what you like) with her message and her brand. It's also a form of word of mouth advertising, which is the best and most effective kind of marketing there is for making sales. Followers and consumers in general, especially us ladies, place a lot of emphasis on word of mouth and what our friends say about a product.

Then there is the other side. Former Australian model and Instagram influencer, Essena O'Neill, quit social media because it didn't represent real life and she felt it was fake. She claimed all her photos were staged and that she promoted products that she personally would never use or wear. All the more reason why influencers need to stay authentic and real with their followers and only promote brands and products they actually like and use themselves.

'I don't believe everything I see in the media, except the ideal body standards, which I unconsciously strive for.'
~ *Natalie, sixteen*

Move Over Monika

Think of online influencers, YouTube sensations or big Insta names you like or follow. Do they have an impact on you? In what way? Do you look up to this person as an expert or role model? If so, why?

Yes, I loved it! it's awesome!

It is one of the most powerful marketing moves Monika makes. Word. Of. Mouth. When girls like something, they tell others. You know how us girls like to talk! If we buy the product and proceed to tell others about it, that's bonus points for Monika.

But you also do something else way more valuable for Monika and the brand. *You sell it for her.* By telling others how much you love your recent purchase, it has a ripple effect. You become a referral machine for that brand, spreading the word. This is the bullseye of marketing. Monika has reached the peak point, the position of influence. She no longer has to work at gaining your attention all the time. Girls now just come to her. She'll still keep up with her efforts but she can afford to be more selective now in how she spends her time.

This is a win-win situation. The customer, you or me, is happy. They share their experience and it allows others to perhaps find a solution to their problem too. The brand grows and reaches more people. Monika (and marketing) at their finest. Have you recently purchased something and told your friends how great it is? That's word of mouth in action right there!

Er, no thanks, that sucks!

The great thing is, if you don't have a good experience, you still tell others. This then has a negative impact for the brand and can damage Monika's reputation. Sales can suffer. As consumers, this is a powerful tool to use! That's why it's so important, if you buy something that fails on its promise in some way, you let the store or the brand know. The same goes for a service. For example, a meal or a take-out lunch. *Yuck!* – tastes nothing like the display portrayed, or how it was described to you. It's up to you to say so. Return it and either ask for a refund or something in else in its place.

You have made two important achievements here. Firstly, you have not settled for poor service and misleading marketing moves on Monika's part. Yay for finding your voice! Doesn't it feel good? This customer feedback is gold. If Monika knows her business, she will take it on board, make necessary adjustments and ensure it never happens to you again. Secondly, you are encouraging the brand or service provider to up their standards and hopefully prevent this negative experience recurring for some other unfortunate customer.

Hitting that bullseye! (AKA reaching target markets)

Why are social media influencers so helpful to Monika and her marketers? Because they offer targeted marketing. No, this has nothing to do with Target, the global retail giant. Targeted advertising means Monika can speak directly to the audience she wants to connect with, get to know and possibly sell to.

Monika's target market (also called audience, tribe, customer avatar) are her followers and community, some of whom will become her customers. They like her stuff and feel inspired by her, so they follow her. Monika will have a different target market, depending on the type of product she is promoting and selling.

For example, if Monika is looking to tell people about her cute little giraffe baby grows for newborns, she will seek out mum bloggers, parenting pages and lifestyle influencers. That's why you wouldn't see this. She's not targeting teen girls. On the other hand, advertising for the latest smartphone or teen app will certainly fall into your feed. You are in the target audience, and will receive lots of exposure and opportunities to see the ads, read reviews, try demos and interact with the product.

A target market is an essential part of Monika's work. It's a bit like you having a few different groups of friends, except Monika's friends vary greatly in age, not just interests. It helps Monika get specific about her message and not waste her time talking to someone who would never in a million years be interested.

The rules of engagement

Social media influencers don't always have to have a tonne of followers to be useful. It's also about engagement. Interaction. Conversation. Involvement. This is what Monika is all about. You are part of the smartest, most informed teen generation to land on this planet. You have also turned Monika's marketing world upside down. Old tricks of the trade no longer apply. She needs to keep up.

Engagement is how Monika keeps up. This is Monika's goal. Online, that includes likes, comments or shares. Offline, that means in-person interaction like sampling, loyalty cards and so on. Monika places emphasis on these areas, because they pay off. Here's how that happens. Because engaged followers are more involved, they are also more likely to spend money when a product that is being promoted. An influencer with a million followers who only sees 100 of those followers actually interacting with a post happens to be less valuable to a brand than an influencer with only 100 followers, but where all of them are engaged. It's a matter of what proportion of the followers are consistently interested in what's going on.

In Australia, transparency laws help keep you safe as a consumer, which is reassuring. However, there will always be a few that fall through the safety net. There's an organisation called the Australian Competition and Consumer Commission (ACCC), which created a best practice guide for brands and bloggers, with penalties for those who talk up products and services, without bothering to mention that they're being paid to promote.

Monika's back-up support

Monika is such an attention seeker! It's in her nature to want to be the centre of attention all the time. She wants you looking at her, listening to her. Ultimately, that's what all of Monika's marketing friends want. Your attention and your friendship.

We talked already about how Monika gets your attention. But it's a busy world we live in and there are so many Monikas vying for your attention. Sometimes when one Monika wants to make an extra push, it calls for back-up, some slightly biased tactics - otherwise known as propaganda techniques.

This sounds somewhat extreme, I know, but it's important we talk about it. Propaganda is often used in a negative sense, when someone uses false claims to persuade you to their way of thinking. You may have heard of political leaders using propaganda campaigns to boost their popularity. In media and marketing, it's commonplace too, though not always negative.

Propaganda can refer to any communication that aims to persuade or promote certain views. It's basically a biased conversation. Monika and her gang will encourage and influence you to think or act a certain way.

These propaganda tactics are powerful. They impact pretty much every purchase decision you will ever make. In other words, every time you buy something, you will be influenced by certain conditions. Among them will be Monika's promises. It helps when you know what these tactics are. Why? Because you can then make a more informed choice about what it is she's saying. It's always best to see the two sides to a conversation, look at the picture from different perspectives, and test what you're being told.

You are the target audience of advertisers. Monika is reaching out to you all the time. She always has something to say to you, remember. It helps if you are aware of this and prepared to handle some persuasive conversations she will have with you. Here are some of the more popular, sneaky, not-so-sweet propaganda tactics you need to know about.

Glowing generalities

Monika's marketing team uses glowing generalisations when powerful feel-good images and words become associated with their product. It's a generalisation when Monika implies that, by using the product, you will be fitter, slimmer, healthier, more beautiful, sexier, [insert magic solution here]. You might have seen fast food advertisements lately where beautiful, healthy, fit teens are in the great outdoors, picnicking on the beach, playing volleyball or surfing, and having a burger.

By default, fast food appears healthier when consumed in the surrounds of a healthy environment by fit, active people. Hmmm, naughty methinks. And not very realistic.

The bandwagon

This comes from the phrase to 'jump on the bandwagon' or to join in with everyone else, just because it's popular and everyone is doing it. This little Monika move plays on the desire we all have to belong, to be part of something, to join a tribe. Of course, it will always be in your best interest too… At least, she thinks it is. (Have you noticed she always does?)

So you may hear phrases like, 'Everyone loves it!' or 'Australia's most popular'. These words seem obvious to spot and you may be thinking, *'Yeah, yeah, I can catch those a mile off'*. But they still work! The reason being, when we hear the message often enough, we start to associate that brand with the title it claims - unconsciously or by default.

Brand-bashing

This is low on the proper etiquette scale and can vary from name-calling and criticising a rival brand to out-and-out 'we are the real thing' claims. You see brands like Coke and Pepsi play this game, often implied without using words. They use images to imply superiority over one another.

You might see something similar in politics during elections when opposing teams have a 'mud-slinging' campaign and try to damage each other's reputations. If Monika is doing her job well, she is confident and authentic in her message and doesn't need to use such dirty tactics. Worth noting but not using.

Product endorsement

We talked a little about this already. A celebrity, musician, sports hero or any well-known public figure promoting a product or service. It's quite the norm in Monika's world. Said 'famous' person gets paid a lot of money to be seen associated with a particular brand. It's a win-win: the celebrity gets paid and the brand attracts more followers, then buyers, because the public also starts to like it.

Why do we like it? It creates a connection or common interest between us and the celebrity, via the brand. From Katy Perry drinking Pepsi to Nicole Kidman spritzing Chanel No 5, from Taylor Swift's preference for Diet Coke to Rihanna wearing Cover Girl, there are so many. At the time of writing this book, Russian-born tennis star, Maria Sharapova, is the world's highest paid female athlete, endorsing everything from apps to candy lines, and collecting sponsorship deals with Nike, Avon, Evian, Porsche and Tag Heuer. Hers is a face that sells a lot of product!

Future pacing

Also known as the 'king of language patterns', future pacing is like visioning and positive thinking, which we'll talk about later in the book. It's a feel-good move. Often, listening to Monika, you might feel like anything is possible. This usually happens when future pacing is at play. You are transported to a 'better place' where all your worries and problems disappear. This approach can be super effective for selling products and services.

First, Monika recognises where you are in your life right now. 'Do you suffer from a lack of confidence?' 'I know you're doing your best' 'I understand your frustrations with your parents'. Phrases that say she recognises and understands what you're going through.

Next, she helps you imagine yourself having solved said problem and how much better your life would be. This is the future pacing part. 'Imagine 10 days from now, when your skin is glowing and your friends comment on how beautiful you look'. For this book, future pacing might look like me saying, 'Imagine how amazing it will feel to be in control of your decisions and confident that the choices you make are the best ones for you.' Lite 'n' Easy uses a version of this in one of their ads, with a happy customer saying, 'I have my confidence back again and I feel great.'

After identifying your future desired place, Monika acknowledges how this would feel for you. Just like how she acknowledged a 'before' the experience or purchase, this is the 'after'. She might say something like, 'That would be life-changing' or 'Wouldn't that be a huge accomplishment for you?' For this book, I might say, 'That would be a huge step towards a more confident you'.

It does make sense for Monika to use this approach if she's trying to connect with you on a deeper level. It's also relevant for pricey high-ticket purchases like holidays, cars, and expensive clothes. You're not going to experience future pacing so much for everyday purchases like basic food items. It can be easy to get caught up dreaming about the future with this one, so be realistic and stay aware of what you feel is possible when you hear this kind of tactic.

Move Over Monika

Think of a time you experienced one of Monika's propaganda techniques that we outlined above. Maybe it was future pacing, where you were reading an ad or an article and you were transported into a future scenario? Or perhaps you have seen a brand compare itself with another brand and position itself as being better?

These master influential moves are not suspect or frowned upon. They are popular Monika moves and (for the most part) come from a genuine place of wanting to help. When they are done well, we may not even be aware of them. However, now that you're aware of some of the deeper psychology behind Monika's moves, you can pause and think, 'I recognise what's going on!' Then avoid rushing a decision without some proper consideration.

The power of awareness is that you get to question the media influencer
and make up your own mind whether it's right for you.

To help you stay sparkly clear and amazingly aware of media influencers all around you, I've created a Magnificent Me Manifesto for you. You can print out your copy from your Action Kit, which you can access at www.helenroe.com/girltribes. Post it on your wall, door or locker, somewhere you'll see it regularly. Then snap a photo of it and hashtag #GirlTribes to share your magnificent moment!

So far, you're getting on well with Monika. There's been more to her than you might first have thought, right? Next, Monika's going to share with you one of the most impressive ways she gets to know you really well and in such a short space of time. It's a growing phenomenon that we all experience.

magnificent me manifesto

My brand choice or lack of brand choice is not my personal identity.

My personal choice is my power. I will always exercise my choice.

I'm smart and savvy, and aware of how social media and advertising can trigger me.

Fitting in is about me feeling comfortable in my skin and staying true to me.

I stay curious at all times and ask questions before I make decisions.

'New', 'sale' and 'must-have' are words that should carry a warning sign.

I challenge what media portrays, because I have an opinion and it counts.

I love myself enough to know that models in the media are not a true reflection of society.

My number of Facebook likes and Instagram followers is not an indication of my worth.

I am aware of Monika and her marketing mob. Although sometimes she's here to help, I can challenge her and make my own decisions.

I feel confident in my choices and can check in with my Do I or Don't I? Checklist questions when I'm not sure.

I don't have all the answers or the solutions. Nobody does. Including Monika.

I continue to challenge (and often ignore) marketing messages.

I find courage every day to be the best version of me.

Part 2

YES I CAN!

Empower Your Great Self

Chapter 5

Ditch Your Fear of Missing Out

Picture this scenario. You're at home on a Saturday afternoon and you scroll through [insert favourite social media feed]. You see posts, photos and videos of all your friends having an amazing time at some party you either didn't get invited to or chose not to go to. You so wish you were there!

You're experiencing feelings of being left out, seeming an outsider, missing something fun or important. Fear of missing out. FOMO.

♥ In this chapter, we take a look at the growing social phenomenon that is the fear of missing out. What's the big deal? Do you have it? And how does Monika use FOMO to get to know you? Once you learn to spot it, I can assure you, bad days can be flipped like a switch and life will only get better. We'll also look at why attitude is everything. Plus, I've got a dare for you that you just have to try!

So FOMO. Sound familiar? Wikipedia describes this common feeling as 'a pervasive apprehension that others might be having rewarding experiences from which one is absent'.

OK, wait. Let's look at that again. Basically, it's having thoughts that others are having a better time than you. That you might miss out on something great by not being somewhere. 'Somewhere' being online social or offline in person. It comes down to experiences. You value creating and sharing memories just as much as having products and possessions. Hence this feeling of missing out on an experience is heightened.

This social angst is characterised by 'a desire to stay continually connected with what others are doing'. Don't panic. You are not alone. It's experienced by over 70% of millennials, the generation of people now aged 18 to 34 years.[2]

It can extend well beyond your disappointment at missing that party on Friday night or the latest update on your Facebook feed. This anxiety that others are having a great time without you can affect how you feel and the decisions you make.

Tell-tale signs you have FOMO

♥ A will-not-go-away urge to stay continuously connected to your friends online. (No, you won't die if you disconnect, trust me).

♥ Fear of being at home, left out, when everyone else is doing something. (Home alone is awesome. You get to have the remotes all to yourself!)

♥ Saying, 'Yes, I'll be there!' even when you don't really want to go, just in case you might miss something fun. (Who said that? It just came out of my mouth, without me even thinking about it!)

♥ Constantly checking your phone because you never want to miss anything. (That's the 22nd time and it's just been a minute.)

♥ Always watching TV and movies, then talking about the latest one to come out. (Did you hear the latest about the latest? What latest?!!)

♥ Constantly wondering what others are up to and feeling it might be better than what you're doing. (I just know she is spilling all the latest right now!)

---

[2] Harris Interactive Methodology, *Millennials. Fuelling the Experience Economy*, Eventbrite (2014)

FOMO is still a relatively new phenomenon, thanks to the surge in social media. But research and proper detective work[3] shows that FOMO, this desire to stay continuously connected to what your friends are doing, brings with it some not-so-good side effects.

When you experience FOMO, you'll experience lower levels of life satisfaction than normal - *boo!* Your overall mood suffers - *double boo!* Also, you are more likely to use social media before you fall asleep (*nooooooo!*) and straight after you wake up (*put it down!*). Other experiences include feelings of being left out, increased focus on how you present yourself online, feelings of loneliness, inadequacy, unfair judgement of others, increased jealousy of others, and even detachment from family and friends. As if life wasn't complicated enough.

Yikes! Are you getting the impression this FOMO feeling can be pretty harsh? I sure am. Don't worry, though. Once you are able to recognise it (and we'll cover that in a just a sec), you'll be able to kick your FOMO to the kerb!

'I started buying clothes that everyone else had just so I would fit in and look 'cool'. I felt like I had to dress to everyone else's standards otherwise they would tease me and look down on me.'
~ *Olivia, thirteen*

'I just see girls on TV and think, meh, I like the way I am. I don't need to change.'
~ *Sarah, twelve*

What's the harm in feeling FOMO?

Everyone deserves to feel happy, connected and like we belong somewhere. That's absolutely true. But it's when others use this desire, which we all have, to try to get you to do something you don't want or need to do that the problem arises.

---

[3] Przybylski, A., *Motivational, Emotional, and Behavioral correlates of Fear of Missing Out*, Computers in Human Behaviour (2013)

Feeling symptoms of FOMO can cause you to react differently to how you truly would. It's this fear that can make us do what we might not necessarily want to do. And this is the part that can have negative side effects.

FOMO in action

Here's a few examples of how fear of missing out might show up in your day.

♥ You rush into making a decision on impulse without thinking it through fully.

♥ You don't talk a big decision over with a friend, parent or someone else you trust.

♥ You feel left out or alone and make the decision to buy/join in just so you can escape from these feelings.

♥ You want to look smart, grown up and in control of your life so you buy/join in, because Monika says it's a good move.

They all sound kind of *ick* don't they? Not a great reason to do something. If you haven't already, take control of this kind of knee-jerk reactive behaviour. You've got this. You can easily spot when FOMO is around now. And you can kindly show it the door.

'Sometimes I feel left out or jealous on social media. It has happened to me many times.'
~ *Katy, thirteen*

'I think the media portrays reality in an untruthful way. When I see girls online looking amazing and having fun, I feel left out and I wish I could be like that.'
~ *Suzi, thirteen*

How Monika plays the FOMO game

Fear of missing out happens in Monika's world with careful planning. It's one of the most successful marketing strategies Monika and her big brands use to connect with you and your friends. This strategy is simply a plan of action to get a particular result. That result might be anything, including encouraging you to click here, comment there, sample or buy something.

You're interacting and engaging with Monika. Once you start talking and spending time with her, you become friends. This approach is Monika's masterstroke. One of her winning moves. A small but mighty strategy she likes to use when she gets to know you and senses you're interested in being her friend (AKA buying her latest thing).

Monika of course wants you to join her friends and is creating such excitement about it. In fact, you think she might explode if you don't join in all the fun. Right now! She's enticing you by sharing what you're missing out on if you don't become part of it. Monika has set the stage up nicely for fear of missing out. Just a quick reminder: Monika is our representation of the marketing mob, the media messages, advertisements and promotions you see online and offline. Her reason for being is to sell stuff to you.

How Monika sparks FOMO

Monika can tap into your FOMO in a number of ways. Some of these include creating urgency or offering something for a specific period. Another one that Monika loves is encouraging her friends (that's you and her other followers) to share her news on whatever it is she's into at the time. Social sharing creates big juicy FOMO! Have you ever been casually scrolling, and within minutes started to feel down or like your world is utterly boring? Yep, a serious case of FOMO mixed in with some comparison and unrealistic assumptions.

Another way Monika might also trigger your FOMO is by creating scarcity and limited quantities of products and services. When we know something is in short supply, we are naturally more inclined get a move on and wait in line. We talk more about these approaches later in the book.

Six ninja steps to turn your FOMO around and show it the door!

Fear of missing out can make you do things that you sometimes don't even want to do. You let others decide for you. When you can handle this fear, you will feel stronger, happier and better than before. Although managing different types of fear does get easier with practice, it's not something that goes away when you get older. Seize the advantage and get ahead now. Here's how to show FOMO the door.

1. Remember things aren't always what they seem

Social media tends to show the best bits, the highlight reel. Nobody is perfect in real life. Often, what we think of as a 'must' or amazing when we see it online is far from what it actually is in reality. Life is not all unicorns and rainbows. That's just in the movies. It's not reality so keep some perspective.

2. Take a break

Yes, switch off that phone, close the computer. Step outdoors and get moving. Talk with people face to face, rather than texting or emailing. Disconnect online and connect for real. (Take this one step further with a Media-Free Day. More on this in chapter 9.)

3. Be grateful for what you have

Think about the positives in your life right now. There is always someone worse off than you. Being grateful is such a cool mood booster. When we practice gratitude and being thankful, there's no room to focus on anything else other that what we appreciate. It's not possible to be upset or anxious at the same time as being grateful. Pretty good, hey?

4. Go easy on yourself

You are smart. Use any experience of FOMO that rises up in you to help you focus on what it is you really want to do next with your time, money and attention. Did you want to spend all your pocket money on that day out or that outfit? Use your savings and your energy for something you truly want and believe in.

5. Practice saying no

I'm sure you've had experience using this one with your friends or an annoying sibling. But this is not about saying no to a request like 'can you pass the salt, please'. This is about saying no when you don't know why you're drawn to saying yes for no reason other than FOMO. Way more challenging. Practice how you might say no. This creates time and space for what you do want to say yes to.

6. Go JOMO!

Yes, you've guessed it. There's a polar opposite to FOMO. JOMO! Joy of Missing Out. Hooray! JOMO is your best friend, so get to know it really well. When you have JOMO, you are so happy and busy doing your own thing that you have no time to worry or care about missing out on that party, that conversation, Monika's messages. Monika does not like JOMO, by the way, but that's no reason for you not to.

'I often have a laugh with my friends or my mam about stuff I read or see on TV. Sport has taught me how to eat well and look after myself in a healthy way. Some of these diets and scrawny models I think are awful. Being skinny isn't the be-all-and-and-all for me. It's about being well in myself.'
~ *Joanne, thirteen*

Strike your superhero pose

Whether it's a trend, following the leader, fitting in, wanting to be with your friends, peer pressure can be exhausting! 'Everyone else is doing it, so you should too'? Er, no. Feeling obliged to do a certain thing or be a certain way to be accepted and liked? Nope! Monika thrives on it though. This is her green juice, her oxygen supply, her energy source.

What about the times when you are just not feeling it? We all have off-days, the ones where you'd rather push the snooze button and curl up under the covers. But you can't. You've got to show up and get on with it. Or maybe you're doubting yourself, not sure if you can really be this confident, strong person you want to be. It could be a big school presentation, a match qualifier, a first date, musical opening night, exam day, anything big enough to make your palms sweaty and your throat dry.

It's at times like these you need some fresh inspiration that will make a difference. Sometimes all you need is a new perspective. So are you ready? It's time to strike your superhero pose. No, you didn't misread that! But don't worry, there are no SuperMan outfits required for this. Stay with me here...

Strike a pose. Change the physical stance of your body. Research has proven that changing your physicality also changes your thoughts. Get out of your head and expand your body to feel differently. Psychologist Amy Cuddy talked about this in her famous TED talk back in 2012. (It's been viewed over 30 million times – Google it!) She says that when we *pretend* to be powerful, we are more likely to actually *feel* powerful. It's a similar belief to the 'fake it till you make it' phrase you may have heard before, but based on science.

Picture it. You see someone standing with their shoulders hunched, arms folded with a cross look on their face. Would you feel like spending time with them? It's hardly a relaxed, confident, welcoming pose is it? Certainly not a look you want to aspire to before a life-changing moment. Now picture the opposite. A person standing straight and tall, shoulders back, with a relaxed happy smile on their face. What's this body posture communicating? You can't help but be drawn to listen or talk to this person.

If we look at images of everyone from Oprah to Mick Jagger to world leaders, we see the link between power and poise. This is often referred to as 'power posing'. We see it all the time. Watch out for it next time you see the president or prime minister speaking. You may not intend on being the next Oprah (although if you do, go you!), but this is still relevant for you in your life.

Understandably, this is not a move you may be eager to pull in the middle of the classroom. However, it's something you can practice in private. Phew! Reputation intact. Now the research bit. And the part you can do.

If you stand like a superhero privately before going into a stressful situation, it will create hormonal changes in your body chemistry, which in turn cause you to be more confident and in control. You can do this before any occasion where you're feeling a little wobbly.

So what exactly is a superhero pose? It's basically like you see in the cartoons. Standing tall, chest out a little, shoulders back, hands on hips and a relaxed (not cheesy) smile on your face. How amazingly empowering is that? Just think about it. By shaking it up and standing differently, simply holding your body differently, it tells your brain to feel differently too. You can do this in the bathroom, in your bedroom or somewhere else private.

This is tapping into your personal power. *WARNING!* This pose is not going to offer you an instant download of your maths homework! It will not give you knowledge or skills that you don't already have.

Striking your superhero pose puts you in the frame of mind to make the most out of your situation.

You get to create your own kind of power and energy. That is priceless.

Move Over Monika

Give your superhero pose a try! This stuff is grounded in science and it's proven to work. You have to hold your power pose for at least two minutes. No laughing! Feel yourself being really, really, really powerful. Even say powerful statements to yourself while you do it. Depending on the feeling you want to experience, you might like to pick and mix from the selection below.

- ♥ I am enough. I love and respect myself.
- ♥ I can do this. I am a strong, powerful, confident girl.
- ♥ I am ready and do not have to be perfect to be confident.
- ♥ I believe in myself and trust in my own choices.
- ♥ It's OK to make mistakes. I do my best.
- ♥ I am unique. I do not compare myself to others.

How did you go? I'd love to see you in your superhero pose. If you're feeling brave, snap a pic of yourself and post it with the hashtag #GirlTribes. You'll not only fully embrace your power pose, but you will inspire others too! Dare you to give it a go!

Monika, you keep repeating yourself

Remember your grade four teacher writing in red pen at the end of your masterpiece My Summer Holidays essay, 'Repeating yourself too much', because you mentioned swimming, sun and fun 100 times? Um, yes, well, in Monika's world repetition is excellent! Repetition is her middle name. Praise to the power of repetition. Here's why.

If we see something often enough, it creates a pattern, which in turn creates a kind of comfortable reassuring familiarity. These are feelings that Monika and her brands strive to achieve from the audience — familiarity and reassurance. It's the beginning of a beautiful trusting relationship. That's a great place for us to be in a brand's eyes.

Say, for example, you turn on the TV and you see a familiar ad. You're waiting for your favourite program and know this ad always runs before it. You're so familiar with it now, you don't mind it. In fact, you may even like it. Think about the chorus of your favourite song. It's a bit like that. You enjoy the rhythm and repetition. The familiarity makes you want to join in and sing along! I bet you've caught yourself humming along even to seriously annoying ads at some point. I know I have!

Repetition helps learning and can result in greater understanding of a particular brand or product. If you see it often enough, the message starts to become clearer. This is particularly helpful if Monika is telling you about the latest technology or something with a lot of detail.

That sounds and looks familiar

The familiarity principle is an important one for Monika and her marketing team. It's where we have a tendency to develop a preference for brands and products that we see more often. The simple act of becoming more aware of and familiar with a brand makes us increasingly likely to accept it.

Advertisers know that this familiarity with their brand or product can result in you choosing to buy it. In most cases, the most well-known brand wins. In fact, it has been proven that when you are shopping, you're far more likely to buy a familiar brand, even if you have never tried it before.

I remember that!

Repetition is one way of remembering things. Monika and her marketing team call this 'brand recall'. Your long-term memory is where Monika's advertisers want to go. When you can recall a brand or product long after you have seen or heard the ad, you are more likely to choose this brand over another.

There it is again!

I'm sure you've viewed an ad on TV and then later seen the same one pop up online or in a magazine. It's everywhere! Using different mediums or platforms can greatly increase Monika's chances of having her message remembered. When you see an advertisement many times, in lots of different places, you are more likely to choose that brand first.

Ready to take action?

Monika knows that on average you need to hear or see an advertisement at least seven times before you take action and buy. Yes. Seven times! Even when you love what you see. There are lots of reasons why she needs to keep repeating herself. It helps build your like and trust in the brand. Also, you may have been busy the other times, not listening, disinterested or just confused about her message.

Great work, we've cracked the code to fear of missing out and how to change your state of mind by changing your physical stance. Cue superhero pose! And you'll never look at those comments in red 'repeating yourself too much' in the same way again! Don't forget to take further steps with your free Action Kit at www.helenroe.com/girltribes. Now it's time to get our heads around Monika's psyche.

Come and have a nosy into what Monika gets up to when she works her powers of persuasion. These are tried and tested secrets that have been passed on through generations of Monika's marketing family. They pack a powerful punch. You may even want to steal a few tips and practice the art of persuasion on some of your friends! Let's take a look.

Chapter 6

Your Hidden Powers of Persuasion

I don't have to prove anything to anyone.
I only have to follow my heart and concentrate on what I want to say in the world.'
~ Beyoncé

The art of exceptional communication and persuasion is no accident. It takes lots of research, tests and trials and action. Practice. Practice. Practice. And sometimes mistakes too. Shock horror! Even Monika gets it wrong sometimes.

♥   In this chapter, we will dive into Monika's six essentials for accelerating her powers of persuasion. And the impact that has on how she creates a rocking marketing campaign. We'll talk about practices that the top teams use for great results and how you can steal some of these ninja moves to win people over. We'll also look at some of the classic mistakes Monika makes and what she does next.

Let's be honest. It can be challenging getting your attention. In fact, it's the biggest challenge facing Monika and her team right now. Trying to reach you and get your attention amongst all the other clutter, messages and information overload. Monika's goal is to connect with you through all the clutter successfully. There's even a term for it – 'cut through'. Sounds a bit harsh really! All it means is trying to cut through the noise and clutter in the media so you can hear her message.

clutterclutterclutterclutterclutterclutterclutterclutterclutterclutterclutte
rclutterclutterclutterclutterclutterclutterclutterclutterclutterclutterclutt
erclutterclutterclutterclutterclutterclutterclutterclutterclutterclutterclu
tterclutterclutterclutterclutterclutterclutterclutterclutterclutterclutterc
lutterclutterclutterclutterclutterclutterclutterclutterclutterclutte
rclutterclutterclutterclutterclutterclutterclutterclutterclutterclutterclut
terclutterclutterclutterclutterclutthroughclutterclutterclutterclutterclu
tterclutterclutterclutterclutterclutterclutterclutterclutterclutterclutter
clutterclutterclutterclu

In today's society, you are bombarded with so many different messages and noise wherever you look. Advertising creative John Bevins, who built one of Australia's most successful ad agencies, uses the above example to demonstrate the challenge Monika has of getting your attention. Did you spot it in the above paragraph? The message Monika wishes to communicate is hidden in the clutter. Have a look. The words 'cut through' appear on the right hand side, second last line. Monika has to think creatively how she can stand out with her message.

As a teenager, you are one of the most active, stimulated, multitasked, busy demographics in existence. You are also one of the most informed generations. You can trust or verify any decision (purchasing decision or something else) with a quick Google or online chat. This makes for an interesting time for Monika and other marketers trying to attract and keep your attention.

There are a gazillion theories and texts out there on this subject. However, even with all the online advances, Monika works on some basic principles. I want to share these with you because I believe they're also fantastic tools to use in your own life. These are handy skills to help you perfect your powers of persuasion. Give them a try. I can tell you this much: you'll be in for a surprise when you use them and see how you can turn others around to your way of thinking.

These steps are not some scammy quick-fix skills to get you what you want. When Monika and her marketer friends use moves like that, incorrectly, they usually don't work and end up giving the brand and marketing team a bad name. It feels pushy. That's not what we are talking about here. So let's get started.

Six pack-a-punch persuasion points:

1. Reciprocation ~ *You scratch my back, I'll scratch yours*

The basis of reciprocation goes like this: I do something for you, then you feel obliged to return the favour. Tit for tat kinda thing or 'you scratch my back, I'll scratch yours.' We are naturally wired this way. If you do a favour for someone, they tend to feel obligated to do a favour for you.

Monika is using this practice when you see her giving away free samples. It's common to feel a sense of obligation when you receive a free sample. Almost like a type of reflex action, we can feel obliged to then buy that item.

You may have experienced this. Sampling some cheese or chocolate at your local supermarket, perhaps you felt obliged to buy the product? Sometimes we'll go out of our way to avoid this feeling of obligation to reciprocate. Research showed people actually went to the extent of crossing the street to avoid being given a free flower 'in return' for a voluntary donation. Interesting, huh?

> *Move Over Monika*
>
> Think of the last time you received something free, a favour from a friend, a sample in a store, someone shouting you a smoothie? How did you feel after the experience? Do you feel you 'owed' the person back and needed to return their generosity? If you did, this is the principle of reciprocity at play!

2. Commitment and consistency ~ *I say and I do*

No doubt this one sounds familiar. It's a wise principle for achieving success in many aspects of your life. In Monika's world, it's a powerful move that requires patience, skill and an eye on the prize or the end result, when things get tough.

It goes something like this: when we commit to something, particularly in public and in front of friends, we are likely to act in a way that is consistent with this commitment. In other words, if I declare to others that I will do something, then I am more likely to stick with my decision and follow through.

You might see this type of commitment when someone makes a promise or a pledge to get fit, for example. Once they set their goal and declare it to friends or family, they are more likely to act in a way that's going to support their goals, i.e. do the work!

This works well for Monika because, once success is achieved with small actions and commitments, then greater requests can be made. Have you ever entered a competition where you are asked to list three reasons why you love a particular brand? You've just displayed commitment to a brand by listing the reasons why you love it. And yes, I've done this! Years ago, I won a weekend trip for two to Paris from Ireland. Awesome, right? I entered a competition on the back of a jar of Nescafé saying why I loved their coffee. I'm not a lover of this brand today, but that 'you're our winner!' phone call still ranks as one of the best I ever received.

I've used a form of this technique later in this book too. In chapter 9, I'll ask you to pledge your commitment to your Media-Free Day and post it on your bedroom wall or even on social media. That's another form of encouraging commitment and follow-through on your end.

Move Over Monika

When was the last time you committed to an action in front of your friends or family and followed through on your word? Maybe it was a pledge or a promise of some kind. Was it easier to fulfil when you had accountability? We are more likely to follow through on our commitments when we are accountable to others. It's easy to say to yourself, 'Oh well, I didn't get around to it today', but we feel a greater sense of disappointment in ourselves when we have to tell others.

3. Social proof ~ *She says it's great so...*

You know already how this works. We are more likely to go along with or comply with something if we see it's similar to what others are doing or thinking. Simply put, we look to the behaviour of others as a guide to what's appropriate behaviour. And this can be pretty useful, depending on how you use it.

It doesn't have to mean that you're not independent or need reassurance before you make your own decisions. It's just an extra step we take as girls to fill in some blanks and help us make better decisions. ☺

You've probably given in to this kind of influence at some point. Have you ever passed the scene of a road accident where everyone is slowing down and turning their heads to look at the smashed cars? This 'rubber-necking' often continues long after the accident scene is cleared up, purely because we see others slow and stare, so we do too. Monkey see, monkey do.

In Monika's world, social proof is like gold. What *others* say about Monika's reputation is equally important as what *she* says and does. Often social proof can be mixed with other approaches such as the commitment one I mentioned. Wearing coloured rubber wristbands is a popular way to support something like a cause or charity you believe in and also shows you committing to something with your friends together. Bonus points if the bracelets are cute!

'The girls in my class, we all wear hair accessories and so I buy new ones to be part of that.'
~ *Lilly, twelve*

Move Over Monika

Think of a time you looked to your friends or others to see what they were doing in order to help you make a decision. How did social proof help you make up your mind?

---

4. Liking ~ *Yeah, You Get Me*

We call this the 'know, like and trust' factor in Monika's world. In other words, you are more likely to comply with someone and do what they ask, if you already know them, trust them and like them. It helps if the other person shares the same beliefs and attitudes as you do. The more you can identify with and feel some common interest with Monika, the more you are willing to trust her, right? She 'gets' you.

In advertising, Monika or one of her well-known celebrity friends often becomes a role model for brands. She is 'the face' of whatever product she's promoting. She is carefully selected for this role based on what her audience (teen girls) like. So if you see Taylor Swift on perfume packaging, it will sell bucket loads more than a perfume with… *ummm*… me on it! Monika and her brands are also flipping this on its head, as they know how savvy and smart a shopper you are.

I've stuck by this principle myself for many of my bigger purchase decisions. I will choose a brand I'm familiar with and like over another competing brand, even if things like price or promotions make the other brand more attractive at the time.

Building the like factor is not just reserved for recognisable celebrity faces in advertising. Brands will often include the average person, the 'girl next door' in their marketing campaigns. It can make the brand more relatable for audiences. Coca-Cola did this when they printed a range of individual names on their bottles. For fans of the soft drink, it was a huge hit. Monika connected on a personal level with her existing fan-base and likers.

Move Over Monika

How important is it for you to 'know, like and trust' a brand or product Monika is selling, before you purchase it? How does this make your choice easier?

---

5. Authority ~ *Listen up, I know what I'm talking about*

The world is made up of leaders and followers. There are leaders in positions of authority who influence their followers with their message and persuade them to act in a certain way. The fact is we're more willing to follow the instructions and suggestions of someone in authority.

In Monika's world, tapping into this authority by using leading sources, research and experts is helpful. People respect and trust experts. After all, we ourselves cannot be experts in everything so that's why we trust those in authority in their chosen subject. Take uniforms, for example. We grow up trusting and respecting figures of authority. This is especially evident with uniforms and how we perceive people wearing them, like a doctor, policeman or security guard.

There have been numerous studies done that show a man dressed in a uniform (in one case, simply a high visibility vest) gets more compliance for requests made to passers-by, than a man who made similar requests, but was wearing regular civilian clothes! Monika uses this source of power in her marketing campaigns all the time. She might quote research, use expert opinions or involve a well-known credible professional in a particular field to reassure us.

'I don't believe everything marketing says is true. I make myself aware of the motive of the brand... In most cases it's profit. But it's sad to see other, sometimes younger girls and even adults believing everything that they are fed through media.'

~ *Issy, seventeen*

Move Over Monika

Are you more inclined to listen to and believe a point of view if the message is coming from someone in authority? Does it make it easier to trust what that person says?

---

6. Scarcity ~ *Time is running out, get a move on!*

This has got to be one of my favourites! Scarcity is simply a supply of something that is going to end soon. It's an offer that has limitations attached. It's running out! *Ahhh!!* Panic stations and scrambling ensues. We get caught up in the moment and all logic goes out the window.

It's a fact. The less available something is, the more value we tend to place on it. So is this a complete con, saying something is 'limited' or 'last few remaining' or 'try it now before it runs out'? Mostly, it's genuine, but there are some of Monika's manipulators out there (AKA sleazy sales people) who use this technique when there's no limited supply at all and it's completely untrue.

When scarcity is genuine, it works well for Monika. Say there's a shoe sale and you see a pair of those boots you've been dying to get with 25% off. Sweet! You ask if you can try them on and the shop assistant says something like, 'Sure, that's the last pair we have'. I for one would not assume the lady is trying to trick me. I'm all in, already trying on those shoes! That's how I bought my first (and only) pair of red heels. It was a combination of scarcity and social proof. My friend was with me, cheering me on with, 'Every girl has at least one pair of red shoes'. Even though I don't wear them much – OK, never – I still won't give them away!

Move Over Monika

Have you ever purchased something because of scarcity – that sense of it running out and not being there the next time? Remember your motivation when you bought this item. Was it more about the initial thrill of getting it or the joy of actually having it. Often, with scarcity, the thrill of buying is stronger than the joy of continuing to own the product. Alarm bells if this is the case!

Circle back to chapter 2 and remind yourself of the Do I Or Don't I? Checklist before making a big decision.

Now that you've brushed up on your superpowers of persuasion, it's time to put it into practice. Knowledge without action is useless. Next up, we'll look at ways you can use your newfound insights to turbocharge your confidence, and take greater control over your choices and decisions.

Chapter 7

Spread that Word Like Confetti

Dear life, am I doing this right?
And I know that I can't understand
What you hold in your hands for me

~ Delta Goodrem

Now that you're equipped with the six secret pillars to Monika's success and influence, you can start to see and predict the way Monika acts. Which is brilliant. Let's look a little closer at one of Monika's six ninja powers of persuasion, social proof. There's more she has to share.

♥ In this chapter, we take a look at the oldest and most effective way Monika gains popularity and encourages her friends to purchase. Best of all, it's free! In today's digital world, this trick is more important than ever. And you are part of it already. We also see how Monika groups her friends for better results, gets gender-specific and brings those girly colours into the mix. Let's take a look!

When girls like something, they tell others. And they tell others. And they tell others. And the viral effect continues. As we said earlier, us girls like to talk, which Monika often refers to as WOMM or word of mouth marketing. She wants to sprinkle and spread that good stuff everywhere, like confetti.

If brands build a great experience, customers tell each other about that. Word of mouth is very powerful. ~ Jeff Bezos

Why should you care about WOMM?

You may not be raving on and on about how great the movie was, how awesome your new trainers are or how cool the latest app is, but all it takes is one time. Then someone else says it. Just once. Another person adds their opinion. Once. You are a big part of word of mouth marketing, even with just a subtle mention. Handle this responsibility with care!

When you're talking, sharing, posting and commenting about a particular product, you are actively participating in word of mouth marketing, which we know from earlier means you're doing Monika's work for her. Up to now, most of the time, you were probably blissfully unaware. For all you know, it's something interesting and fun to talk about. That's OK. You're not doing anything wrong here. Although Monika will be very pleased with you indeed! ☺

Taking this a step further, Monika will actively encourage you to share your positive experiences about her latest *thing*, especially if you've got great examples and stories of yourself using/wearing/eating that item. This is what we want to hear. Is it any good? Will that hair curler work on my fine hair? Does that top suit my figure? Will that bra fall apart in the wash? It's kind of helpful when we have answers to these questions from friends we trust. They've been the guinea pigs, tried and tested the product you're thinking about, so now you can buy it (or not) confidently. That's good news all round.

Because you know how powerful your word of mouth is now, it's a timely reminder to proceed with caution. Choose carefully. Only endorse, talk about or support brands and products that you use and love, or would like to use. They should also match up well with your values from chapter 2. Monika will encourage you to share your comments with friends, often with a reward or prize to be won. Again, go for it if it feels right do so. You are not a marketing machine and you don't have to regurgitate brand benefits for the sake of it. It's still your word, your choice.

Aahhh! When things go viral!

News travels. We all know that. Everyone loves a good story or a good reason to buy something that will make their life easier, happier, healthier or whatever. Monika knows this, and oftentimes will start out with a piece of news that has the sole intention of making it go bananas, reaching crazy amounts of people.

Take YouTube, for example. Monika has friends, sometimes not even in marketing, who upload fun stuff that goes viral. Millions of people crack up at the sight of the world's best skateboarding cat (yes, over 7 million) or the talking twin babies (over 134 million – yep, I thought I read that wrong too!). It's fun. It's a distraction. It's an instant mood-changer. A very important resource.

Where Monika comes in is that she then approaches these popular channels for advertising and endorsements. We've talked about this earlier in chapter 4 with the online influencers. Traffic online equals an opportunity for Monika to get her message to more people.

Keep in mind, too, that Monika will try to kickstart a viral campaign. But often it's down to luck and what the audience takes to. You, the public, control the outcome. A great example of this working effectively was the Australian public safety video a few years back called *Dumb Ways To Die*. It has over 92 million views and the campaign won numerous awards worldwide. It was viral marketing at its most ingenious. Other personal favourites of mine include the Evian Baby (96 million views to date) and The Dove Real Beauty Sketches (64 million views to date). Google them, they are worth a watch.

Move Over Monika

You've probably been part of viral marketing, viewing and liking your own favourites. Think of a particular example where you shared or talked about something, either online or offline. Were you happy to contribute to the marketing of this product? Did you support the brand values and the message it delivered? It's good to answer these questions and know why you share, like or comment. It gives meaning to how you're contributing.

Practice what you post

You've seen the power of word of mouth, so this nugget of wisdom has evolved since my mama told me to practice what I preach. I've seen, and I'm sure you have, Personal Brands who supposedly represent an 'ideal' then in reality live a lifestyle that contradicts it. That Personal Brand may or may not be endorsing the product for money, but either way, it becomes a case of double identity where the online persona is quite different to what they're like in real life. Maybe they are 'sometimes' practicing what they post, but not in a realistic daily living way. If what they post is the one and only day they feel amazing, love life and have it all together, but in reality they have more days where their world is just ordinary, they aren't practicing what they post.

Aside from losing every thread of respect for yourself, it just doesn't help anyone if you're pretending to be someone other than yourself online. If you're striving to be Miss Perfect, then go write a novel and create that character in a *fiction* book, or go act it out in drama club.

Who do you want to be at the end of the day when your head hits the pillow? That's the person you have to be comfortable being around. Can she have a real life face-to-face conversation and say the things she says online to a real person? Is she proud of how she supports her friends and sticks with them, through thick (lots of likes) and thin (no likes)? Let your online friends see the real you. In today's hyper connected online world, genuine, authentic and real presence is what really stands out.

Connect, don't compete

OK, I'll be the first to admit it. I'm the competitive type. Ever since that tiny tots race (exasperated because I didn't win the handbag!) and all through high school, university (except first year undergrad, where I got a little side-tracked) and my corporate career, which was male-dominated and competitive rather than collaborative. Dark suits were my monotone work wardrobe for a decade at least. It was driving me to be a better person. Or so I thought. But it wasn't until recently when I started working in my own business that I realised it wasn't serving me well.

Business, life and Monika's world is not war. It is not about *me*; it's about *we*. How could I collaborate and work with others, grow and learn if I saw everyone as competition? Just like life, business is all about relationships. Connecting is a big part of this. Monika has shown us this throughout our journey together too. Coming from a defensive, contracted energy space is draining. When I flipped this to look at how I could collaborate and work with (not against) other women, I started having some fun too! No two people have the same strengths. Together we are stronger!

Then there was the comparison. This buddy goes hand in hand with that competitive mindset. Together, ready to create havoc. A fair amount of research has been done on female competiveness. Why do we compare, compete and cut each other down? It seems we do it to make ourselves feel better, a form of self-promotion and protection.[4] What's happening is we're competing with ourselves, not other women. These distorted misconceptions we have of others are nothing more than a reflection of what is going on inside of us. It's just easier to turn on the other girl and find fault with her.

---

4   Vaillancourt, T, *Females Using Aggression As Competition Strategy*, Royal Society Publishing (2013)

Monika loves this. She is all over it. She gets that you, her audience, have to relate to the person in her message. You are smart, and like we've mentioned, you place huge weight on word of mouth.

What you say versus what you think

What we say aloud can often be at odds with our internal dialogue. Monika can have a great influence on our thoughts, without us even realising it. That's the subtlety and skill of great marketing. We are going to take a breather from external influences right now and step back from the Monika's world of media marketing.

A great way to get a true impression of your thoughts on life and all the things that fill your busy mind is to write a letter to your future self, the you 10 years from now. A message in a bottle, if you will. No digital versions allowed. Good old-fashioned pen, paper and an envelope. Go let those words spill out onto the page. Do a word vomit. No holding back.

Here's a suggestion of some things you could ask yourself. Where do you see yourself in 10 years' time? What worries you the most now and for the future? What are you grateful for? What makes you happy? What are you really good at? Who are the most important people in your life and why? Keep going, write everything that comes to mind. Then seal the envelope and keep it somewhere safe. Better still, give it to someone you trust and ask them to post it to you in 10 years' time.

I'm in on this too. But to keep it relevant for you, I'm going to flip it round. I've written a letter today, speaking to my younger teenage self. OK, here it is.

Dear Helen,

You've wanted to be 'older' ever since you were little. Funny that. When you finally get there, a fully-fledged adult, you want to be young again. So as your wiser older self, right now I want to say to you 'slow down!' I am so proud of you and I'm here to tell you that you can relax now. It's all going to be just fine. This complicated life is actually great fun, but it can be even better if you keep these few things in mind.

First up, please know that where you are now is OK. A teenager, discovering, learning and adjusting. Just be where you are. I understand you hear this a lot, but let it sink in this time. Stop living for tomorrow, when you're older, smarter, more beautiful or more popular. Hint: it doesn't make these things happen faster. It just means you don't get to enjoy who and where you are now.

And that tall, lanky frame that you're impatient and reluctant to inhabit? It's strong and healthy and serves you well in years to come. Love the body you are in, my dear one. The harder you resist the more it reminds you. Relax yourself out of this resistance and into acceptance. When you accept yourself, you are freed from the burden of needing others to accept you. Confidence and acceptance are clothes you wear for a lifetime.

Your strong healthy body, you may not see the value in your skin right now, but miracles await. It gifts you two girls, little miracles. You compete in sports like a true champion and you find your freedom there. Follow that for as long as you love it.

You do have a competitive streak and it drives you to all kinds of perfectionist tendencies. This is - um, what can I say? - a real pain! You know what I'm talking about. The conversations that go something like, 'I'm not cool enough', 'It's not perfect enough', 'It's not ready yet', 'Who am I to do that?'

Well, I'm here to tell you to let it go. You are enough. Yes, keep growing and learning, but in the moment, when you do your best you are enough.

Illness doesn't call often, but when it does, it calls with a clear message. Slow down. What's with all this rushing? Quit it! You are chasing the horizon and you know what happens there. You never actually reach that point. And that's OK. You are here for the journey. Who you become in the process. There is no 'getting there'.

You are great at supporting others, my dear. But do you back yourself and believe in yourself as much as you do other people? Practise backing yourself first, because it will allow you bring more to the lives of others. When you believe in yourself and love yourself, only then can you bring a happier healthier you to the world. Your friends and family will thank you for it.

I don't want to give too much away, but you do meet your soul mate. Your fierce independent self takes you through many interesting relationships. It's amazing and fun and really hilarious at times! Just know that you can enjoy each experience for what it is and let go of Miss Perfect a little. Also trust your gut feel. It never lies.

Keep mutual respect in all your relationships and you will thrive. When you are being you is when great things happen in your life. That time you won the gold in the U12 nationals in the 600m? Do more of that. You were on fire, girl. You had the vision. You put in the work and you showed up, meeting the universe at a place called fulfilment, achievement and joy.

Mum always taught you to say thank you. Practise gratitude every single day. Especially the days where you feel you have nothing to be thankful for. When you feel gracious and recognise what you do have, there's simply no room for negative or lacking thoughts. It keeps your energy and vibration high and you continue to attract more awesome things in your life too!

Most of all, my dear one, have fun. It's an amazing journey you are on. Everything turns out wonderful. And more. Keep your vision and your dreams alive. You have great things to contribute to this world.

All my love,
Your dearest older self,
Helen

Move Over Monika

What might your letter to your future self say? Perhaps there are some parts of mine that inspire you? Write yourself a letter to your future self in 10 years' time. Seal it and put it somewhere safe, or give it to someone you trust to post it back to you in 10 years.

She shops how she wants to shop

Monika has come a long way. What she gets is that females buy completely differently to males. We are wired differently. Therefore, we buy differently. Hallelujah! It's official. That's why you never take a guy shopping, right? Over the years, advertising has evolved greatly, from the 'I give my man Gatorade' ad (Google the Checkout channel on YouTube for the ridiculously sexist approach of sixties advertising and also learn why you should never drink that stuff again!) to the Always #LikeAGirl unstoppable ad, watched over 38 million times on YouTube.

Getting back to the way we shop, it's recorded countless times in science that the female brain functions differently to the male. Thankfully Monika and her marketing buddies are recognising the rising power of the female consumer (that's you!), both amongst teens and adult women. So how exactly are females different in how we buy? Here are just some of the obvious ways us ladies like to do things.

♥ **It's no longer just pink and pastels.**

Her

Pretty packaging may catch our eye, but females are more interested in building a rapport and trust in a brand, before we invest in what Monika has to offer.

Him

Prefers functional, simple and less detail.

♥ **Engagement is the new enticement.**

Her

Female buyers want to talk to Monika and ask questions about why she thinks her product is the best choice. We like to share our opinions and say exactly what we feel.

Him

Yep, I'll take one of those.

♥ **Let's shop around.**

Her

And this is not just an excuse to spend longer shopping, right, ladies? It's in the name of research and waiting until our decision 'feels' right. We make more of a zigzag around the shopping centre, then usually end up back where we started.

Him

Lateral thinker, single focus with no distractions. Left-brain logical rationale. Easiest, fastest route to the checkout.

♥ **Enjoyable and fun!**

Her

She enjoys the bigger picture, holistic experience, collective and with friends. Word of mouth plays a big part of that.

Him

No so much. Strategic thinker, purpose-driven and less into the 'experience'. Makes a beeline to the jeans department, grabs his size and buys them.[5]

Monika and her teams of marketers do mountains of research every year, segmenting consumers like you and I into groups and analysing why we buy. The female teen segment you belong to is an important one. This leads us to gender marketing, a big growth area for Monika and the brands she represents.

His and Hers: Gender Marketing

Segmenting the marketing into pink and blue, along clear male and female audience lines, has allowed Monika and her marketing friends to sell more and charge more. It offers more variety, choice and tailored products for each audience. But it wasn't always like this. Did you know that way back blue was actually first promoted as the colour for girls because it is delicate and dainty? And it was pink for the boys! Ha!

In the 1980s, LEGO was gender neutral. Yep, I got creative with combos of blue, red and yellow LEGOs in a time when toys didn't scream blue or pink. The iconic LEGO ad resurfaced recently with the four-year-old girl dressed in jeans and a t-shirt proudly displaying her creation and the caption 'what it is is beautiful'. It's a great example of what advertising should be about, in this case the creative expression of the child. For its time, it was progressive and controversial having a girl in the ad. It's all changed now as a kaleidoscope of bright pink and purple LEGO Friends launched in 2012, scored the company a massive 25% increase in sales and tripled their little female customers.

There's many more brands upgrading to be more gender-specific for the teen and adult markets. Some ideas work and some don't. Some take it too far and get caught out. Recently, Nurofen were brought to the Australian Federal Court. Thanks to the great work of the Australian Competition and Consumer Commission, Reckitt Benckiser, the

[5] Barletta, M, *Marketing to Women, Second Edition*, Dearborn Trade Publishing (2006)

makers of Nurofen, were fined \$1.7 million for breaching consumer laws and misleading consumers. Their range of 'pain-specific' products, including Nurofen Period (complete with pink box), all contained the same ingredient and did the same thing. They still made substantial profits from these products, however.

Some brands are doing a great job of gender-specific marketing. Bodyform's No Blood Should Hold Us Back campaign really does power through the period stigma of historical advertising in female hygiene products. This category remained a challenge for Monika's crew, until now. No more daisies or scientific blue liquid. This ad shows real girls keeping active during their period. With real blood. It's been viewed more than 5 million times. Worth a look.

So whether it's bread for women's wellbeing or Bic pens in pink florals, make sure you're aware that pretty packaging and promises aren't always a reason to buy something. Do your research.

Move Over Monika

Ask yourself: are you buying a product because it says it's for teen girls? Check out the alternative and see if there's a difference. Most likely it will just be in price and pretty packaging.

What once used to be 'for the whole family' has turned into a busy segmented market. There will always be some new shiny 'just for girls' product to try.

Next, we jump into Monika's masterful work on our minds. Getting inside our minds is much easier these days, because Monika has so many opportunities 24/7. You on the other hand will have to keep close guard on who you grant access to enter. It's time to explore your neighbourhood.

Part 3

LEAVE YOUR LEGACY

Take Awesome Action

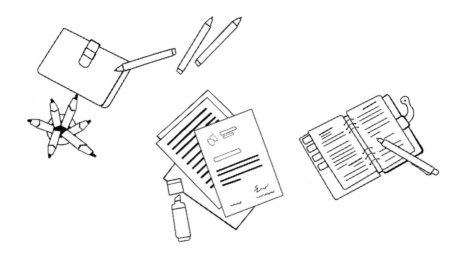

chapter 8

'Mind' Your Own Business

All the people who knock me down only inspire me to do better.

~ Selena Gomez

If the inside of my head were a neighbourhood, it wouldn't be safe to go there alone at night. When author Elizabeth Gilbert said this, I cracked up laughing. It's so true. Our minds are often the craziest place to be! We say all kinds of harsh things we'd never dream of saying to a friend. It's amazing how we can talk to ourselves and think it's OK, yet we wouldn't dream of speaking to those we love the same way.

♥ In this chapter, we check out your inner mind, your neighbourhood and how you can make it a calm and inviting place. A confident and empowering place where you can create and check in on your dreams and your visions. We'll look at how you can stay positive and make those dreams a reality, all while Monika does her thing.

Minding your own business isn't about keeping your nose out of other people's business. It's about looking after the health of your own *mind* and what goes on in that busy brain of yours. Be so focused on improving yourself and minding your affairs that you have no time to worry about what others are saying about you. Let's talk some more about how you can do this.

Lucy loves music and is a big Taylor Swift fan. She dreamed of meeting Taylor and got so close twice. Then it happened. Her dream became a reality. Really. Here's her story.

'I had wanted to meet Taylor Swift ever since I was seven years old. At the first Taylor Swift concert, the Speak Now World Tour in 2012, I got one metre away from Taylor, when she ran through the crowd. At the second concert, The Red Tour, my mum and I got aisle seating so Taylor was going to walk past us during one of her songs. Taylor was so close to holding my hand but then I got pushed away by a bodyguard.

My mum had been bugging me to read this book called *The Secret*, which is all about the Law of Attraction and positive thinking. I always thought, *'All right, Mum and her crazy motivational books'*, but then one day, she sat me down to watch *The Secret* documentary. After watching it, I thought, *'Hey, this is actually really cool'* and decided to try it out.

I started to really put my mind to meeting Taylor Swift. There were 76,000 people packed into the ANZ Stadium for her next sold-out show, including one of my best friends Kealie and me. We had been dreaming about this concert for a good year, and had spent that year creating these crazy costumes and trying to get noticed on Tumblr, so Taylor would know we were coming to the concert.

We had both saved up hundreds of dollars to pay for VIP tickets in the front few rows, an amazing hotel room near the stadium, fuel and costume expenses. From the moment we walked out of our hotel room to the concert, we were stopped for photos with total strangers, which was very surreal. Our energy and excitement were so high, and I couldn't believe I was seeing Taylor again and getting a chance to meet her!

During Taylor's concert, her management walk around the venue looking for big fans with crazy costumes that are screaming the lyrics and dancing like maniacs. They choose about 20 to 30 fans to go meet Taylor for free after the show, in a place set up at each concert called 'Loft 89'. Needless to say, Kealie and I were definitely doing that and had the costumes down pat! As soon as Taylor came on stage, we completely lost our minds. While I was screaming the lyrics of I

Knew You Were Trouble, a woman from Taylor Nation (Taylor's social management) came up to us and asked us if we had ever met Taylor.

When we said no, she invited us to Loft 89! We could not believe our eyes when she put the Loft 89 wristbands on our wrists and handed us the meet and greet pass! It didn't feel real until I actually met her. Taylor was everything I thought she would be: kind, beautiful and down to earth. Something I'd been working towards for so many years had finally paid off.

I won't lie, part of me thought it was just a series of coincidences, maybe I was just lucky. But when I look back, it was because I was specific with what I wanted. I visualised and dreamed about what I wanted, worked hard at it, kept faith that life was going to give me something good one day, even when things weren't so great. I am so grateful that everything turned out that way it did.'

~ *Lucy, fourteen*

Amazing, right? So maybe you're not a Taylor Swift fan or have no desire to meet a celebrity. What's your dream? What do you want? More than anything? To win the basketball championship? To finally overcome your fear of speaking at school rostrum? To sing at your local drama club? To dance in front of an audience of hundreds at the end of year show? To be insanely happy? Get really clear on your vision, your dream. Only then can you start to visualise it.

Take it one step further. Focus in on one specific dream, one goal. Build some sense of reality around it, almost as if you have achieved it already. Tell a friend, share your dream with someone who cares. For a moment or two every day, picture yourself doing or having what you want. Just like Lucy, your dream can only become reality when you focus on it and move towards it. Small steps that lead to big changes.

Capture your dreams on a vision board

You may have heard of vision boards or dream boards. Capturing a vision of your future dreams and life in words and pictures. There are numerous benefits linked to the science behind this kind of powerful, visual, positive thinking. (What you see you believe.) It's very similar to what Lucy did in our story earlier. You capture images associated with your dreams and goals, motivational quotes, places and people who inspire you to make it happen.

Your vision board is a creative mix of images and words to represent your goals. It is so satisfying to *see* your vision, your dream, in front of your eyes. It also anchors in those feelings your vision board evokes. You could include your personal values from chapter 2, so it's helpful to know these before you get creating. Maybe you want to feel brave, confident, invincible, calm, funny, smart? Really notice how you feel when you think of your dream, then anytime you feel disconnected from this you can come back to your vision board and reconnect.

'I can dream. Who knows what will happen. My dad says everyone should have their dreams!'
~ *Carly, fifteen*

Seven easy steps to create your dreamy vision board

You can make your board online with Pinterest, Picmonkey or Canva, then print it out in colour for your wall. Or do it the old-fashioned way and cut out images from magazines, then stick them onto some poster board. If you feel like rolling up your sleeves and getting gluey and glittery, this one is more fun!

You'll need a poster board or large piece of card, magazines and images from computer print-outs, your drawings etc., scissors, glue sticks, lots of coloured texters. And if you're feeling flahulach (pronounced fla-hoo-lock, it's Gaelic for generous and flamboyant), then some glitter glue!

Here's the general process, but feel free to adapt it to your own version. There's no right or wrong way. Just have fun with it!

♥ Make a list of what you really really reeeeally want to happen in your life. Your vision.

♥ Find and cut out images and words that you associate with your dreams. Positive vibes only. So for example, for personal happiness and joy, I have a pic of a girl having a great big belly laugh.

♥ If you love an image/quote and are not sure why or what goal it ties into, put it in there anyway. It will make sense later.

♥ Edit your images. Go through the pile and decide which ones you want to put on the board. It's likely you'll have some to spare.

♥ Now lay them out on the board and start sticking.

♥ Add your images, written words and personal commitments (like your Personal Brand values or your Magnificent Me Manifesto).

♥ Add any extra doodles or sketches (or glitter glue!) to finish off your masterpiece.

♥ Display your vision board somewhere you will see it and connect with daily. Remember to keep it fresh and relevant. Update it during the year or as you reach a milestone.

I know, you're dying to ask. 'C'mon, do vision boards really work?' Yes! Yes! And yes! Everyone from high achievers, celebrities, top athletes, world leaders to extraordinary entrepreneurs practice some form of visualisation with positive thinking to make their dreams a reality. I even did it for this book. Among other visuals, I have a picture of working with teen girls on my vision board, and also one of a gorgeous book, where the pages are sprinkled with sparkling white light. (Gotta have me some sparkle!) When I see these images, I feel motivated, excited and on the right path. Now it's your turn. What are you waiting for?

Get on it! If you haven't already, go create your vision board, using the seven steps above. Then take a picture and share it with us on social media with the hashtag #GirlTribes, so we can see your amazing work! As Seth Godin our marketing guru says, 'Do what you believe in. Paint a picture of the future. Go there.'

Where does Monika and her world of marketing fit into all of this? She has a pretty powerful mind, so much so that we can often feel she is reading ours. Your Digital Footprint that I mentioned earlier, it's a fast track to your personality and your habits. Monika has at her fingertips state-of-the-art strategies to understand how you behave. This is now the world we live in.

By understanding your thoughts, Monika can then tap into your more vulnerable side. Your negative, self-doubting thoughts. The ones you try to keep to yourself. She's playing on your insecurities. This is not necessarily always a bad thing. When we have problems, we need solutions. Tick. Monika does her job. But other times, you may just be having a bad day, then you see a stream of advertising, YouTube videos and even ads on the back of buses on the way home. Your problem has now escalated into a fully blown life crisis.

FEAR of the unknown

Fear. Do you feel it sometimes? Of course you do, because we all do. In Monika's marketing world, this can be disguised as so many other emotions. Fear of not fitting in, failure, rejection, rumour, the unknown future. The list goes on.

Sometimes you might feel like you want to 'forget everything and run'. Now, this may be something you need to do if you are in physical danger. Just like you need to pull your hand away from a burning stove, fear in the face of real physical danger helps keep you safe! But that's not the type of fear I'm talking about. I'm talking about fear of something that hasn't happened yet. Or may never happen. Fear that you might get left out, disappoint someone or humiliate yourself. But what if you looked at fear from a different perspective?

Let's imagine fear was the acronym FEAR. Flip it and turn it into a positive. FEAR is really 'false evidence appearing real'. Or we could say FEAR is an opportunity for you to 'face everything and rise'. Fear is not fact. It is based on something that 'might' happen in the future.

So why do we spend so much time worrying about or avoiding situations because of things we think might happen? Sounds to me like a sad waste of your talent and time. And Monika knows this. I talked before about how marketing taps into your vulnerable spots, right? Well, this is another one of those times. That's not to say that you should not feel what you're feeling. Yes, recognise what's going on for you and be present and aware. Only then can you make a smarter choice about what to do next.

My mother told me that fear was not an option.
I was always told that women are stronger, so I believed it.
~ Diane von Furstenberg

So what can you do to keep your neighbourhood, that mind of yours, safe? Your mindset and all its mix of chaos and calm. Well, lots of what we've covered in earlier chapters will help. Staying strong and confident in your decisions comes down to the conversations you have in your own head. Your thoughts.

Your thoughts play a major part in determining who you are being. Your thoughts determine what kind things you say and the type of conversations you have. Your thoughts determine your mood and the actions you take. Yes, thoughts are powerful things.

You may be familiar with this cycle of thoughts. Your thoughts become your words and what you say, which in turn become your actions and what you do. This can be wonderful when you're having happy thoughts. You feel great! But it's not as easy when we have thoughts that are not so nice and we believe them. We tell ourselves negative stories and can start to feel anxious, angry, confused, afraid and so many other emotions. The battles with thoughts that go on inside our minds are not reality. They are stories we tell ourselves and often torture ourselves with.

Stressful feelings arise when we resist against reality or particular circumstances. We think the reality should be different to what it is. This conflict is where the tension and stressful feelings arise.

No-one can control circumstances; these are events that happen outside of our control. For example, it rained while you were walking to school. This is a fact, a circumstance you cannot change. What you can change is your thoughts about it and how you respond. Or maybe you keep seeing Monika in this advertisement everywhere, looking amazing. Now you feel insignificant, boring and dull and can't help comparing yourself. You cannot control how Monika shows up. This is a circumstance you've got no control over. But you can control how you respond, the thoughts you have and how you act after having those thoughts. Let's look at this a little closer.

Doing 'The Work'

Imagine if you could turn a difficult, annoying or upsetting situation around for the better. Flick the switch and go from feeling *meh* to *oh my!* Switch from out of control to in control. Sad to happy. Anxious to relaxed. How amazing would that be? You could do this when Monika and her marketing moves get you down or bother you. You could even do this when your younger brother drives you nuts, when you feel hurt or let down by a friend, or when you're alone, feeling a bit sorry for yourself.

What is it? It's an amazing exercise called The Work by Byron Katie, embraced by millions of people around the world. (Used with permission from Byron Katie International, www.thework.com).

With The Work, you ask yourself some simple questions about the reality of the particular situation that is bugging you. You learn that the reality is not as bad as we tell ourselves it is, and your mind becomes more peaceful and accepting of the way things are. Heads up. You have to be patient. And present. No running ahead with your thoughts. Stay in the present moment.

There are two steps to The Work. In the first step, you write down a judgement about a stressful situation in your life. In the second step you ask yourself four questions about that judgement. Grab a pen and paper and let's give it a go.

Think of a time when you were really upset with someone. Picture yourself back in that moment. Bring to mind the thought you were having. Now write down your judgement about that stressful situation. To get you started, here are some common thoughts from girls that might sound familiar to you.

I feel inadequate when I see pictures of pretty girls online.
I wish they would stop teasing me.
School is boring.
I use social media too much but can't help it.
My sister is smarter than I am.
She stole my best friend.
My parents never listen to me.

Next, ask yourself these four questions.

1. Is it true? (Yes or no. If no, move to Q3.)
2. Are you really sure that's true? (Yes or no.)
3. How do you feel when you believe that thought?
    Does the thought make you happy or sad? Where do you feel these feelings in your body?
4. Who would you be without the thought?
    Close your eyes and see yourself with that person, in that moment, without the thought. What's it like now without that thought?

Each question helps you look at the belief from a different perspective and replace it with a more positive thought and feeling.

Now turn the thought around. What is the opposite of that thought? Perhaps instead of 'I feel inadequate when I see pictures of pretty girls', you could say, 'I feel like myself when l see...' or 'I feel confident when I see pictures of other pretty girls and I know I'm unique'. Try saying 'I', 'me' or 'my', instead of the other person's name in your thought, if it's about someone in particular.

The Work allows you to accept yourself and where you are, without changing the reality or circumstances (which you can't anyway). You give yourself permission to find the answers within yourself. This may sound 'out there' at first. How on earth are you supposed to know all the answers? This work is not asking you to be the next Einstein. It's simply giving you an option to trust your own judgement and also look at that judgement from a fresh perspective with a new set of eyes.

It's a powerful exercise and takes some practice. Don't worry if it seems a bit confusing to begin with. You may need some help to work through this the first few times. I encourage you to give it a try. If you would like to access more information on this great tool, you can download the teens worksheet on the resources page at www. thework.com.

It's now time to peer into Monika's world of marketing when it makes a real difference for good in the world. I do love when Monika performs at her best. Making a difference in the lives of others can be taken to new levels when Monika works her marketing genius. It's changing the world for the better. It's your chance to change your own corner of the world and make a real difference too. Let's have a look how.

Chapter 9

Marketing Making a Difference

Success is liking yourself, liking what you do and liking how you do it.

~ Maya Angelou

As you've got to know Monika better, you've seen how she's capable of being actually very sweet and doing some great work. Media marketing is a powerful tool and, when used for the good of others, can have outstanding impact.

♥ In this chapter, let's take a closer look as some examples of Monika working her marketing magic for the good of others. Monika is the ultimate communicator and cool connector. When she brings people together, she can make a real difference, impact lives and inspire fresh new thinking to tackle and alleviate many of the world's problems. This is sure to get Monika in your good books. She can't wait to share some of her success stories with you.

Even if you don't have plans to be the next Malala Yousafzai (an activist for female education and the youngest ever Nobel Prize winner), you still have the capability for great change. This ability alone is so empowering. It's your secret superpower. It could be something as simple as passing a compliment and making someone's day to fundraising for a local cause in your community. The best part is that you get to do something worthwhile by being yourself and speaking your mind.

Start small, with your own Compliment Campaign. Maybe you've heard of this idea. Anonymous surprise compliments are written on a piece of paper and placed in a book or in someone's bag. Just think how good it will feel to bring a smile to someone's face and maybe even make their day. Who doesn't love a compliment? You could take this online too and reach more people. It doesn't have to be anonymous; that just adds a little more mystery to it! Perhaps you could blog about a topic that you love and could talk about all day.

'Girls can do and be anything they want. They are smart and can achieve anything.'
~ *Anna, thirteen*

'Girls make their own choices and decide what they like themselves. We are just as strong as boys.'
~ *Jennifer, fourteen*

Social media offers a global platform to get the word out about key issues in our lives. Important matters, like the availability of education for all children, equality for women, relationships and family life, poverty, homelessness, and health and wellness.

You could use your social media platform like actress Riley Matthews of Disney's *Girl Meets World* did. She wrote an essay about the importance of intersectional feminism, where issues like racism, sexism, oppression and homophobia are addressed together. Her post went viral, racking up more than 97,000 likes on Instagram. She also spoke at the UN Women's annual summit in June, where she explained how gender inequality affects youth. Now that's using media to make real impact.

Businesses use Monika and her marketing efforts to generate revenue and contribute to worthwhile causes. In Australia, Roslyn Campbell is the founder of Tsuno, a social enterprise selling disposable sanitary products made from bamboo fibre. Tsuno partners with charities to help empower women in the developing world. Fifty percent of profits from all Tsuno sales go towards supporting women in the developing world through projects such as the International Women's Development Agency. How inspiring and awesome is that?

As a junior in high school, Megan Grassell took her younger sister shopping for her first bra. Appalled by the experience, lack of choice and over-sexualisation of the padded, wired and push-up options, she decided to do something about it. With her own hand-drawn pattern on her dad's yellow legal pad, her first Yellowberry bra was born. Today Yellowberry is a thriving brand encouraging girls to dream big and know they have the support to do anything.

The Harry Potter star, Emma Watson, UN Women Goodwill Ambassador works through media to promote gender equality and equal pay for women. 'Women want to be women. We just want to be treated equally. It's not about man-hating.' Changing your world starts here, with you.

Press pause on constant connection

Press pause. Take a break from online and offline media. Even in the middle of all this greatness where social media and marketing is doing good in the world. Why? Continuous connection and being constantly 'on' leads to busy, overactive minds and poor mental health. Yikes. That's fact. Research indicates a host of side effects with excessive online use, including stress, sleeping disorders and depression.[6] Even if you think that may not happen to you because you're careful, listen up. Excessive online side effects do not differentiate. Symptoms will not bypass you because you're using media to help you through a rough patch.

You can still stay connected with your friends online. Just be mindful and recognise how much time you actually do spend on media online and offline. If you don't already, try establishing boundaries with your media usage. Create times when you don't use media and allow

---

[6] Mission Australia, *Youth Survey Report,* Mission Australia (2014)

yourself to just be. Doodle, have a face-to-face conversation, exercise, create or be curious. Pick something you enjoy and do it without the distraction of media.

Start with small changes. No doubt you have heard of avoiding the bright blue light before bedtime (meaning no technology in the bedroom). Well, it's for good reason. Neuroscientists have proven that blue light emitted from our phone and iPad devices interrupts our body's natural day-night rhythm (the circadian clock) suppressing levels of naturally produced melatonin in the body. Melatonin is the body's natural hormone that helps control our sleep patterns. No melatonin, no sleep.

Move Over Monika

Challenge yourself to go a day without media. Encourage your family to support you and do the same. Switch off. And notice how different things are. At the end of the day, write down how you felt. You can download your My Media-Free Day Playsheet at www.helenroe.com/girltribes. Be sure to pick an accountability buddy, someone who you can share your challenge with and celebrate with (OK, brag to) when you've done it!

Perhaps it might feel strange, calm, slow, quiet. All quite normal. Or maybe it will feel new, exciting, peaceful and freeing. Give it a chance. Don't make judgements about it until the very end of the day. I bet you will be in for a surprise or two!

When you're back online, post your ahas and share your experience with the hashtag #GirlTribes. And so we can congratulate you and cheer you on!

---

my media-free day

Today, I impressively declare that I will give up all media and technology use for a *full day*. This includes the use of phones, iPads, television, radio, magazines, newspapers and any other media product in disguise.

Signed:_____   Date:_____

Complete the questions below at the end of your day.

1. List three things you didn't like about your Media-Free Day.

2. List three things you did like about your Media-Free Day.

3. How did a Media-Free Day help you be a better version of yourself?

When Monika helps a good cause

We've looked at some examples of great people doing great things with the their voice to change the world for the better. Another way some brands can do great work in the world is to partner with a non-profit organisation for a good social cause. This is called cause marketing. It's a bit like Monika doing voluntary work at her local Vinnies. It's good for her reputation and also it spreads the word. As you know, Monika talks to lots of people.

With cause marketing, you the consumer (the person purchasing) can feel you are contributing or making a difference in some way, by buying a product that promotes a good cause. There is a mutual benefit and a win-win for both players in cause marketing. The brand gets further exposure and their name associated with a good cause, which in turn helps their audience connect with their brand. Which essentially means their followers or fans totally admire what they're doing and love them even more.

The non–profit receives great publicity and awareness it would otherwise not have access to, which essentially means they get the word out more effectively (i.e. good marketing) and many more people get to learn about the work they do, in turn helping them help more people. Non-profit humanitarian organisations get a new lease of life, funding and credibility by being associated with a trusted brand.

There is no better way for Monika to play and build her fan base (loyal customer following) than through a brand's alignment and association with a worthy cause.

A great example of this is TOMS brand shoes that donate a pair of shoes to a child in need for each pair purchased. Their tagline is 'we are all connected' and empowers its customers to help a child in need when they purchase a pair of TOMS shoes. They've also branched into eyewear, with part of the profit used to save or restore the eyesight for people in developing countries. And there's great ways you can get involved. There's ventures such as One Day Without Shoes and Style Your Sole, which help make fundraising and awareness interesting and great fun too!

In Australia, the wonderful Zambrero Mexican food chain has a humanitarian focus and partnered with Stop Hunger Now, an international hunger relief agency. For every burrito or bowl you purchase, a plate of food is donated to someone in need. At the time of writing this, over 8 million meals had been donated to those who need it in Africa, Asia and the Americas.

Another fantastic Australian example is the social enterprise Thankyou, whose mission is to end global poverty by selling a range of natural body care products (which I love and are all over my house). After Thankyou's costs are taken care of, they give 100% of their profits to the trust, which then distributes the funds to life-changing food, water, health and sanitation programs around the world. And you can be part of it too. When you purchase a Thankyou product, you receive a unique Tracker ID and you get to check online the details of the project your product is assigned to fund. This blows my mind.

Now Thankyou is challenging the billion-dollar baby market. This is one of the most competitive markets where leading brands spend up to $10 million on marketing. (Check out the Thankyou crowdfunding video on their website. It will make the hairs on your neck stand on end).

I happened to be working on the NIVEA Baby launch in Europe years ago, when we battled with the competition to enter the market and give consumers a choice. Unfortunately, pantry-filling tactics (price promotions in-store that encourage customers to stock up so they don't need to buy the new product when it launches) really challenged the brands survival. Check out co-founder Daniel Flynn's book *Chapter One* that raised (at the time of writing this book) $1.2 million dollars to fund the new Thankyou baby range. You can still buy the book and fund the future.

Have you seen these thoughtful partnerships and cause marketing at play? You may be familiar with bigger causes like public awareness campaigns for breast cancer. Perhaps you've noticed it when you purchased something and a percentage of the sale price went to a particular cause.

Product (RED) created by U2's Bono and Bobby Shriver is a licensed brand that seeks to raise awareness and funds to help eliminate HIV in Africa. It has partnered with many brands including Nike, Apple, Gap, American Express, Starbucks and Coca-Cola, to name a few. Each brand creates a product with the Product (RED) logo. Then 50% of the profit is donated to The Global Fund. Since its establishment in 2006, and at time of writing, (RED) has contributed over $350 million to support The Global Fund HIV/AIDS.

There are some pretty amazing examples of marketing to make a difference, right? I'm sure you've got some of your own that you could add. So we've looked at Monika and her marketing team doing some really great work. Work that serves a need, offers a solution and creates positive change.

This is *not* to be mistaken for philanthropy, even though cause marketing and philanthropy may appear the same. Philanthropy is when a brand or business *donates* funds to their chosen charity or cause. That's also a great way to make a positive difference in the world.

Pura Vida Bracelets are a wonderful example of this. What started as a college trip for two Californian friends to Costa Rica turned into a global business that supports over 190 charities today. Griffin and Paul happened across two bracelet peddlers, living in poverty. They took home 400 of their beautiful colourful friendship bracelets, and placed them in a bowl in a local boutique. Within days, they were sold out. People were asking for more. A movement much greater than the bracelets themselves had begun. Pura Vida, Spanish for 'simple life', serves as a reminder to people all over the world to slow down and enjoy the moment. Pura Vida is also a member of One Percent For The Planet. They donate 1% of their annual net revenue to environmental organisations worldwide.

Monika shies away from fast fashion

As we've seen, Monika does represent some great brands that practise social responsibility and sustainability. Many of Monika's friends have a conscience about the products they buy and where they come from. The infamous 2013 Bangladesh Rana Plaza building collapse and subsequent loss of 1,100 lives put western retailers on the map for all the wrong reasons. The UK cheap chic chain Primark and Italian brand Benetton were among the many manufacturers based in the Rana Plaza, operating with varying levels of safety, and questionable work conditions and pay.

Are you buying your clothes from sweatshops? It's not always easy to tell once a shiny new garment is hanging in a window display. A sweatshop is a factory that violates acceptable working conditions, including unfair wages, unreasonable hours, child labour and a lack of benefits for its workers.

Sweatshops do not help the poor by giving them a job. Most workers barely have enough to spend on food for their families. And because, according to dosomething.org, the majority of sweatshop workers are women, some employers force them to take birth control so they can avoid supporting maternity leave and other health benefits. Not OK.

Makes you wonder where the clothes you buy actually come from, doesn't it? With so many stages in the manufacturing cycle, it can involve a bit of detective work too. So what can you do? Well, if you're buying a t-shirt for $3, it's safe to say the person who made it hasn't been paid a great deal to make it, right? Alarm bells. It's also worthwhile to think, at times like this, about quality over quantity. Do you really *need* more clothes?

Not sure where your favourite brand makes their clothes? Write to them and find out or look on their website. Even better, ask them on social media. Ask the question: what do you do to ensure decent working conditions in the factories where your clothes are made?

If they are made in Bangladesh, you can also ask if they are part of Accord, a legally binding agreement between brands and trade unions to protect the rights of workers. All ethical brands should have an ethical sourcing code that's available to the public. If they've nothing to hide, then they will openly share the manufacturing locations they use.

The non-profit Clean Clothes Campaign is dedicated to improving working conditions for workers in the global garment industries. They get the message out to consumers, companies and governments, plus they support workers and their right to better working conditions.

Nearly all of the clothes sold in Australia are imported[7], with China dominating the market. Some brands have publicly committed to improving work conditions in this 'fast fashion' world where 'pile them high and sell them cheap' is the motto. In 2005, Nike became one of the first brands to publicly release, in full transparency, their list of suppliers, followed by Levi's and H&M. To date, Kmart is the only Australian retailer doing so with Target committing to the process.

---

[7] Castle, J., *Ethical Clothing: Where Did You Get That Outfit?* Choice.com.au (2014)

> *Move Over Monika*
>
> Be curious and dig for some answers. Ask the brand on your clothes where they were made. Join the Fashion Revolution and use the power of fashion to change the story behind the people who make your clothes and accessories. Here's what you can do. Take a pic of you with your clothes tag showing, post on social and ask the @[brand] #whomademyclothes. The future of fashion is in your hands.

Make up your mind, Monika!

This next Monika move is quite an advanced strategy. I saved this until last because it's the killer, confusing move that gets most of us. Monika says she's your friend, is so nice and then turns around and tells you to change the way you look or the way you laugh. Call it double standards, a blatant contradiction or just plain confusing.

Monika does tend to contradict herself a lot. She's ever so nice, paying you compliments. These are usually future paced, which look something like 'you will look amazing when you use [insert product that you 'should' be consuming/wearing/eating]'. She's regularly offering suggestions on how to improve yourself and your life. And she loves to make others feel better about themselves by saying things like 'respect individuality' and 'be yourself'.

But isn't that a contradiction? Monika and her friends (AKA marketing peeps) are telling you to try this and do that, while at the same time saying it's OK to be yourself, unique and different? Unless you have a clone, that's impossible to do.

So why would Monika do that? Firstly, because when Monika shares a worthy 'feel good' belief with you, like you being unique, she connects with you on a deeper level. You feel you know her and like her a little more. You trust her a lot sooner and possibly to a greater degree too. Plus, often, she genuinely wants you to feel good about yourself. We are naturally drawn to be with friends and people who make us feel good about ourselves. When Monika establishes that level of connection and trust, then she can start making suggestions and recommendations for you.

Monika's 'I've made it' badge of brand-loyalty

Brand-loyalty is the elusive, hard-won badge of honour for Monika. We talked a little about it earlier. It's a badge that tells us that she's reached a level of 'know, like and trust' with her friends and customers that they will only associate with her for that particular experience. Brand-loyalty is the 'I've made it' badge of marketing. Monika earns this badge when she has done her job properly. Connecting with you in such a way that is unforgettable.

She'll know when she's earned her badge and you will too. You will feel like Monika just knows you. You may even feel like she's a best friend. I remember my first time experimenting with makeup. It was a natural clear lash mascara. I was taking baby makeup steps (and rightly so). For many years after that, I was completely attached to that brand, even though I grew out of their products. I always associated it with my first makeup experience, feeling like the brand understood and cared for my needs at that time. Monika well and truly earned her know, like and trust 'I've made it' badge. I was loyal to her brand for far longer than I might have been without that association.

It can be an enjoyable, rewarding and fun experience when you have a favourite brand. There are so many ways you can associate with a brand you love; it's not just about buying the product. You can join their community of followers online, share stories or experiences. Often, a brand offers a free resource of some kind, maybe an online magazine or a YouTube channel. It's always handy though to be aware of your attachment and relationship to a brand. As my mum likes to say, 'It's good to have your wits about you'. Once you both have reached the 'know, like and trust' in your relationship, things tend to move along much more swiftly. Monika can progress to the fun stuff!! Telling you what to buy, wear, eat, do, and listen to – in short, who to be! Sometimes - and this is OK - without realising it. Monika has an amazing skill of listening to you, understanding you and wanting the best for you. Except for one thing. She omits to mention that the best for you is also the best for her. This is when she moves from marketing and sharing ideas and solutions into sales, where she asks you to buy.

Sales and marketing: peas in a pod?

Up to now, we've talked about Monika and her marketing moves. Sales and marketing are like peas in a pod. They work together and often hang out together. There is a strict difference though. Monika works in marketing. She attracts the right people, tells the story and builds relationships. She speaks to many. Monika does not do sales. She could, but really it takes a completely different skillset, so it's best she leaves that to someone else.

Sales is the work that is done after Monika has left the scene. Sales can sometimes be given a bad rap. It's seen as being pushy or icky, but that's only when sales jumps ahead, before Monika has had time to work her magic. It's a straightforward sequence. Monika works on her marketing, speaking to many people. Next, sales arrives and works on an individual one-to-one basis.

Think of it like a romance. Marketing is flirting. It' all about getting to know you, sharing stories, what you like and what you don't like. A bit like window-shopping, you haven't made up your mind. Sales is dating. Taking it a step further. There is commitment on both sides (hopefully!) and a stronger bond has formed. It's happily ever after (again, hopefully!). Sales and marketing do overlap; it's never straightforward. But what relationship is?

Move Over Monika

Have you got a particular brand or product that is your clear favourite? Now that you've seen how marketing can make a difference, does your favourite brand meet these standards? Maybe it's giving back in some way, empowering girls to be themselves, inspiring creativity or really helping brighten your day. Whatever it is, be aware why you have such brand loyalty and attachment to the brand. And if you don't have a particular favourite, that's absolutely fine too.

Next we turn into the home straight, the final chapter, where you get to come home to your GirlTribes. That feeling of knowing where you fit in and finding your tribes who accept you and *get* you. It's never straightforward, but as you know, nothing worthwhile ever is. Doors are ready to be opened. You just need to knock. Let's go!

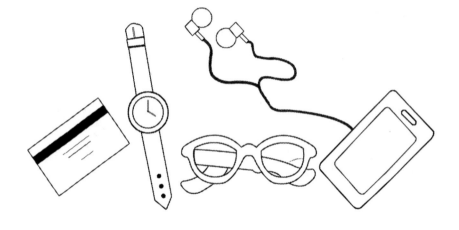

Chapter 10

Coming Home to Your GirlTribes

When I'm with you, I'm standing with an army.

~ Ellie Goulding

I've lost count of the number of tribes I've been part of over the years. Depending on what stage in life you're at, you seek and find each other, settle in and get comfortable. There's something quite special about surrounding yourself with people who *get* you. At times, you might have a few different tribes, for different interests. But they all flow together, supporting you as you bob along a more enjoyable, smoother sail.

♥ In our final wrap-up chapter, we come home to your GirlTribes. We look at how *you* can influence Monika and make a real impact in the growth of meaningful brands and businesses today. Let's challenge the status quo and what media portrays is a good fit for you. You have everything you need to create something far greater than yourself. Onwards.

Which tribes do you feel called to join? Who do you follow and friend, and how do they define you? Or perhaps you are paving the way towards creating your own tribe, with your own message and mission? Monika will invite you to use a brand or be associated with it by interacting with it or following it on social media. You're ready now to make an informed decision about where you want to be seen and who with.

In the old days of Monika's marketing, it was a matter of mass marketing with an average message for the average person. Mass media reached lots of people with the same message. It was broad speak and general. TV, press, radio and outdoor advertising (billboards) all desperately tried to connect with the right people. It was somewhat targeted but still very much like throwing mud at a wall and hoping some of it would stick.

Today Monika's conversations are targeted, with a special unique message. Meaningful and specific. It's no longer a one-size-fits-all approach. Audiences, tribes, you and I are seeking meaningful marketing and meaningful products.

We are interested in things that matter.
Products that tell a story and services that connect real people.

When we buy something, we want to know where it came from, who made it, and how sustainable it is. The focus is on 'we' not 'me'. We expect a two-way relationship. We are challenging Monika for transparency in her work and full disclosure about how she does things. You are the first generation to interact and engage with brands extensively and in unique new ways, compared to previous generations. This means you get to make more impact. You get to influence and inspire the brands and businesses of today. It's an amazing opportunity to support what you believe in, exercise your voice and your power of choice.

No-one is excited by normal. And that's great! It means there is something out there for everyone. And if there isn't, you can go create it. If selling colourful odd socks can be a multi-million dollar global enterprise then you can certainly find your own kind of weird. It's the age of connection, conversation and co-creation. You get to be part of the brand story. It's an empowering time for you as a consumer in Monika's world. Embrace it and run with it.

Keep out of the clone chamber

Although I often joke about cloning myself so I could be in two places at once, it's actually happening already. Much of social media and the online world, including Monika's marketing one, can be unoriginal. Monika's ideas, messages and marketing moves are copied and repeated. Certain marketing principles work and that's why it's easier to make a copy than create an original.

It starts to get murky when people (rather than systems) decide to clone themselves from other success stories. Becoming a social media clone might even happen unintentionally. You follow a brand, live and spread their story, becoming a clone of them. It's a bit like spending a lot of time with someone who has a different accent. You might start to introduce a few similar intonations and inflections here and there in your conversation. Before you know it, you're *speaking* like them. (OK, I'm an Irish girl living in Australia for several years and this has not happened entirely, but I do catch myself sometimes with hints of an Aussie accent creeping in!)

The world doesn't need another echo.
It needs your voice and your unique impact.
It needs your unique Personal Brand.

You can't achieve this by being exactly like someone else. Revisit and revive your unique Personal Brand and your core values. This is your unique DNA that will keep you aligned and connected with yourself. It will also help you navigate Monika's busy world. We are all still figuring this life out, and where we fit in, so if needs be, adjust your PB (Personal Brand) along the way. Just make sure to have a point of reference, a benchmark. And remember, please, please, please, keep out of the clone chamber.

Stay true, because Monika might try to change you

I'm afraid it's true. Monika will always have an answer for you, the next big thing, the latest. It links back to the 'not enough' and 'needing more' sentiments we talked about in chapter 1. It's not all bad news though. Some of the change is good. We all grow older, change and evolve. What we liked last year may not be what we like today.

After years of playing scholarly Hermione Granger in the Harry Potter films, Emma Watson was uncomfortable coming to terms with being seen as a sex symbol and people always wanting to change the way she looked. 'If I do a photo shoot, people desperately want to change me – dye my hair blonder, pluck my eyebrows, give me a fringe. Then there's the choice of clothes. I know everyone wants a picture of me in a mini-skirt. But that's not me. I feel uncomfortable. My idea of sexy is that less is more. The less you reveal the more people can wonder.'

No doubt you've heard the saying 'the only thing that's constant in life is change'. But that doesn't mean you have be someone you're not. Revisit your Personal Brand values and measure your choices against those. Your own personal navigation system.

Change is sometimes needed to better ourselves. Looking forward to the future and building on what we have achieved is all part of our journey in growing into who we want to be. But a word of warning: Monika will advocate change, upgrades, new stuff, whatever it may be, all the time. It keeps her in business. You do not always need to keep up with everything she says. You can run your own race. Agreed? Good.

Why? Why? Why?

I'm sure when you were little you asked lots and lots of questions. I know I did. Young minds are inquisitive and have no filter. There's never not a good time to ask a question. Have you noticed that with little ones? And they keep repeating the question until they get an answer! From 'why is the sky blue?' to 'Mummy, why is that lady picking her nose?' to 'why can't I?' Well, it's time to be a kid again. Get curious and start asking why, why, why?

OK, so your teachers might not like this one. Monika probably won't either. It makes her job a little more challenging. But in the long run, she creates better quality brands and products that meet her tribes' needs. Questioning why something is the way it is rather than taking it at face value means your interactions with Monika becomes a two-way conversation. You, the consumer, become engaged and connected with the brand. You are part of the story. Ask why Monika does something a certain way, rather than accepting it's the best way, just because she says it is. There's more than one way to bake a cake.

Now that you've got to know Monika better, how do you feel about her? For the most part, Monika is your ally and your friend. Don't wait to be invited to the party. Contribute to the story and share your thoughts. Demand to be part of Monika's brand story. Whether that's to challenge and change it, or to enhance and elevate it. Shape the story. Your voice and those of your tribes can do that. Challenge the order of events and question what Monika says. Spark a conversation with friends, get others thinking and see where it takes you. This is your opportunity to say how you think it could be. Show up online and face-to-face as the same authentic person. Be the example.

Glowing GirlTribes

Wherever and whomever you choose to grace with your presence, be all there. Know why you are there. Monika will always welcome you. Have fun discovering and learning the ways of the world. Be gracious and know that you can leave at any time. It's always your choice.

If the pressure gets too much, it's usually a sign that something needs to change. Maybe you need to find a new tribe. Your GirlTribe feels like coming home. A comfortable familiar place where you are accepted. As yourself. Surrounded by people who share your values and your beliefs. Your GirlTribes have your back and want what's best for you.

Whether that's online or with friends at school, being with your GirlTribe is being somewhere you feel confident and strong. When Monika shows up, you're able to recognise her, but also respond in a way that serves you, rather than on autopilot. Take your time. Really think things through from all the angles. It may not be what she wants but that's OK. You make your own decisions and show up in a wiser way in your world.

'It makes me feel happy. I just live in the moment and then I think back to it and I smile about it.'
~ *Mary, thirteen*

'If people like me for me, that's fine but I don't expect everyone to like me. Can't get on with everyone. I don't like everyone in my class so can't expect them all to like me back. As long as I have one or two really good friends that's OK with me.
~ *Sophie, fourteen*

Finding your GirlTribes

You might have found your GirlTribes already. Maybe you're still looking. Or perhaps you've outgrown your existing tribe and it's time for change. Wherever you are on your journey, remember you will always be searching unless you first accept yourself where you are. Don't look to Monika's opinion, where she's calling you. Get to know your Personal Brand (yourself) back to front and inside out. Know what you love and what makes you tick. Go be that person. Then you will automatically start to attract the right kind of GirlTribe to you.

It gets noisy in the clutter of online and offline media. (It wasn't easy spotting that cut through earlier was it?) Use your newfound GirlTribe skills to break free from the constant communication. Remember to give yourself a break to get back to reality, check in with some face-to-face friends. Go offline and get active. Reconnect with friends having fun and dare to be uncool!

Accept that some people like different stuff and diversity is a good thing. It doesn't mean your choice is not the right choice. It's just different. Underneath the surface, we're all pretty much looking for the same basic principles. Self-acceptance and belonging. Try not to judge or criticise how others are doing their thing. It takes your attention away from where it should be - on your efforts. Tend to your own garden first and you'll have roses [or insert your fave flower] blooming in no time.

Nurture the marketing ecosystem

Monika and her marketing teams are no longer working independently from you. All great brands are now part of an ecosystem. An environment where they interact and are interconnected with you for survival. Just like in an ecosystem, each organism (including you) has its role to play. Monika needs you. She needs your input and your opinions to contribute to this world. She values your insights and an understanding of what's important to you.

It's a complex community, this marketing ecosystem. We've looked at how Monika gets it right and sometimes how she gets it wrong. New brands can destroy the balance of the ecosystem if not kept in check. This is where you come in. Speaking out and making smarter choices. Challenging why a brand does things a certain way. Questioning ethics and values. Carefully considering following and liking influencers online.

Just like ecosystems, boundaries can be hard to define and often blend into each other. Where are your boundaries? Define what you will and will not do, and put it into practice. Support the ecosystem in ways that align with your values and contribute to brands that make a positive impact to your life and the lives of others.

I hope this book has been more than just words. I hope it's given you greater perspective and a fresh lens to look through into your world. One that encourages you to shape your own unique Personal Brand and how you show up, contributing to worthwhile meaningful marketing. May you find self-assurance and confidence to stay curious and challenge messages the media markets to you.

Enjoy the journey. Go find your GirlTribes. Have fun! Monika will be keeping an eye on you, watching closely. But you're ready. You've got this. Will you choose to make a difference? I'll leave you with that small but mighty question. Media-savvy and ready to make your mark. Let me know how you go!

Big hugs,

Helen
xx

resources to get help

Helplines

Life Line

13 11 44
www.lifeline.org.au

Kids Help Line

1800 55 1800
www.kidshelpline.com.au

Suicide Call Back Service

1300 659 467
www.suicidecallbackservice.org.au

Sane Australia

1800 18 7263
www.sane.org

Websites

Reach Out
www.reachout.com.au

R U OK?
www.ruok.org.au

Tune In Not Out
www.tuneinnotout.com

Youth Beyond Blue
www.youthbeyondblue.com

Mental Health Online
www.mentalhealthonline.org.au

The Butterfly Foundation
www.thebutterflyfoundation.org.au

MoodGYM
www.moodgym.anu.edu.au

Living Is For Everyone
www.livingisforeveryone.com.au

Headspace
www.headspace.org.au

Conversations Matter
www.conversationsmatter.com.au

Black Dog Institute
www.blackdoginstitute.org.au

Printed in the United States
By Bookmasters